TO HONOR OUR HERITAGE

A GUIDE TO PRESERVING LOCAL CHURCH HISTORY

ERIC K. THOMSEN

To Honor Our Heritage: A Guide to Preserving Local Church History

Published by Randall House & D6 Family Ministry cooperatively with the Executive Office of the National Association of Free Will Baptists and the Free Will Baptist Historical Commission. All Scripture quotations, unless otherwise indicated, are taken from the King James Version, public domain.

Design: Eric K. Thomsen | Cover image ©2018 Eric K. Thomsen
Proofing team: Matthew Steven Bracey, Elizabeth Hill, Phillip Morgan, Jennifer Thomsen

---

Library of Congress Cataloging-in-Publication Data

Thomsen, Eric K., 1972-
To Honor Our Heritage / Eric K. Thomsen
Includes bibliographical references and appendices
ISBN (Print Edition): 978-1-614-84165-4
ISBN (Ebook): 978-1-614-84167-8

1. United States—Church History. 2. United States—Historical Preservation.
3. United States—Free Will Baptists.

Available online: www.HonorOurHeritage.com

Printed in the United States of America, 2023

*In honor of the generations
of Free Will Baptists who
have gone bravely before us.*

CONTENTS

"Forasmuch as many have taken in hand to set forth in order a declaration of those things which are most surely believed among us, even as they delivered them unto us, which from the beginning were eyewitnesses, and ministers of the word; it seemed good to me also, having had perfect understanding of all things from the very first, to write unto thee in order, most excellent Theophilus, that thou mightest know the certainty of those things, wherein thou hast been instructed."

—Luke 1:1–4

Introduction

LEARNING FROM LUKE

In the opening verses of his Gospel, Luke the physician peeled back the curtain of time to reveal his motivations and methods for writing. He acknowledged he followed the example of previous writers who recorded "those things which are most surely believed among us." What were *those things*? We find the answer in the first verse of Luke's sequel, the Book of Acts: "all that Jesus began both to do and teach."

In a straightforward, detailed, and thoughtful manner, Luke's Gospel relates the story of Jesus, from birth and ministry to death and resurrection. Luke followed that account with the fascinating narrative of the early days of the Church, from Christ's final command to His followers to the arrival of the Holy Spirit and the world-changing events that followed.

As a physician, Luke offered a unique, intriguing perspective. He emphasized particular and important details (the virgin birth of Christ, for example) in a manner that clearly reveals a doctor's heart. From the opening verses, we also learn Luke wrote with the heart of a historian. He described a clear method for research and historical preservation.

However, beyond Luke's historical intentions, research, documentation, and writing, he simply told a story, the *greatest* story. His protagonist? The hero? A Savior, the God who became human to redeem humanity by offering Himself as a sacrifice for their salvation. In His victory over both physical and spiritual death (the ultimate antagonist), this hero Savior proclaimed victory and procured salvation for mankind. Luke's story can be summed up in a single sentence: "For the Son of man is come to seek and to save that which was lost" (19:10).

In recording this divine narrative, Luke—physician, historian, and ultimately, Scripture writer—modeled a clearly defined method today's writers of church history do well to follow.

- **First,** Luke stated his intention to record an orderly declaration or narration (1:1) of the life of Christ. He wrote with a specific plan toward a specific goal.
- **Second,** Luke explained his narration was based upon the commonly held beliefs of eyewitnesses who saw and heard Jesus (1:2) and then recounted their experiences to Luke or his associates. Luke researched well, sought and found reliable sources, and documented sources for his readers.
- **Third,** Luke stated his intention to use eyewitness accounts to "write unto thee in order," more literally, to record these things *carefully and with method* (1:3–4). Luke was not haphazard in writing this narrative. Under the direction of the Holy Spirit, he chose words carefully and with power.

Building upon Luke's statements, this book provides a step-by-step guide to help churches and individuals create a well-planned, carefully constructed, well-documented account of the story of your local congregation. While the historical record you produce will never be Scripture, it will preserve the ongoing story of Christ at work in His church.

ABOUT THE BOOK

Safety is found in "a multitude of counselors" (Proverbs 11:14). This book follows this advice, drawing on the collective wisdom of individuals with a wide range of professional and ministry experience. Their input on the subjects of producing and preserving local church history was harvested through twelve lengthy, personal interviews.[1]

Page by page, you will encounter practical, firsthand advice from historians, writers, educators, documentarians, denominational leaders, historical archivists, and more. They are quoted freely and frequently. At times, reading may feel more like a dinner table conversation with friends than a resource book. Together, these men and women share their collective experiences to help churches and individuals tell their stories more effectively. To learn more about these contributors, their work, and their ministries, see *Appendix A*.

Though written with Free Will Baptist congregations in mind, the principles in this book are relevant for any church that wishes to record its history for the next generation.

As you begin this quest, follow Robert E. Picirilli's advice that local church history is most effective when it "captures the interest of the whole church."

Start now. Talk about your history. Ask people to bring you historical materials. Encourage people to share their stories. Get *everyone* involved.

CHAPTER ONE

WHY WRITE A LOCAL CHURCH HISTORY?

That thou mightest know the certainty of those things, wherein thou hast been instructed (Luke 1:4).

Before anyone accepts the daunting challenge of writing the history of the local church, he or she should first settle the burning question of why it is important to do so. "Many people would say it's *not* important," Dr. Robert E. Picirilli offers with a smile. The longtime chairman of the Free Will Baptist Historical Commission quickly adds: "While some say the only thing that matters is what we do now, you simply cannot separate the present from what the church has been in the past."

Michael Lytle, CFO of Randall House & D6 Family Ministry, recalls these familiar words: "Those who fail to learn from history are doomed to repeat it." This quip is true for churches as well, Lytle notes. "As culture changes, the church tends to change with it. It is important to be able to look back to where we've been, understand what we have experienced, and determine what is worth fighting for as we move into the future." Ron Hunter, CEO of Randall House & D6 Family Ministry, adds, "Too often, the church crosses the same 'mine fields,' when it doesn't have to walk through them at all." He notes that leadership is ultimately about solving problems, and there is no reason we cannot learn from those who have solved the problems already, with history as our teacher. Matt Pinson, Welch College president, agrees: "If you are going to change, know *why* you change....Do your forebears the honor of understanding them."

Carol Pipes, director of communications for LifeWay, notes, "Local church history is part of our ongoing story. I always go back to the importance of connecting history to the present. All the things we did in our early years influence who we are today. We stand on the shoulders of men and women who have gone before, and we continue building on what God did through them. They carved out a path for us to follow into the future."

This is why an accurate historical narrative of the local church is a high priority, notes Keith Burden, former executive secretary of the National Association of Free Will Baptists: "Future generations will have no appreciation for the rich heritage of your church unless *someone* chronicles its history. And, it is easier to envision the future when you have a correct understanding of the past."[2]

Burden points to another practical, though often forgotten, reason for preserving and publishing local church history: legal issues. On one occasion, the courts called Burden, as a denominational leader, to testify regarding a situation in which a church had been victimized by a "hostile takeover" involving a minister from another denomination. The original congregation sued to retain possession of church property. Unfortunately, the church had not updated records for years and did not follow the mandates of the historical constitution and bylaws closely. As a result, the judge ruled against the long-time congregants in favor of the "new" congregation.

"As a general rule," Burden concludes, "courts make decisions based on the historical documents of the church, specifically the constitution and bylaws. A church either needs to bring the church into conformity with organizational documents or bring documents into conformity with the church. That is why it is crucial to know the historical formation of your church."

Picirilli lists three pragmatic reasons for preserving local church history: First, many people are curious about the history of their church. They simply want to know. Second, a good church history serves to challenge people about what their church can and should be. "When you tell the story of someone who did something well in the past," Picirilli offers, "it challenges the current congregation to follow that example." Finally, a good church history helps the congregation understand who they are and motivates them to remain dedicated to who they are rather than drifting from their tradition.

Like Picirilli, church historian Donald Hughes believes the story of the local church is crucial, because it connects the current congregation to its heritage, gives the congregation roots in a greater tradition, and provides clear testimony to God's ongoing work in and through that particular church in the

**The present may belong to you, the future to your children. But the past becomes what writers say about it.
—Jack Williams**

local community.[3] Best selling author Robert J. Morgan agrees, noting, "Discovering our history strengthens our own personal faith commitment....There is a power that only comes from knowing and understanding our history and heritage."

This clear connection to the past is vital to historian Phillip Morgan. "I'm convinced humans don't truly understand something unless they remember, both individually and corporately. Amnesia is a horrible disease, and it can happen to a congregation if it forgets what has gone before." These corporate memories are crucial for a healthy church and are also a biblical concept. Throughout Scripture, God calls His people to *remember.*

Perhaps the late historical writer Jack Williams put it most simply: "We need writers to preserve our history. Our history is worthy of preserving, and it takes Free Will Baptist writers to do it best. Because there were few written records in early Free Will Baptist churches in the South, much of our history is gone and can never be recovered.... The present may belong to you, the future to your children. But the past becomes what writers say about it."[4]

Phillip Morgan adds an exclamation point to this conversation: "As culture continues to become more secular, both Free Will Baptists and churches-at-large must be more intentional about *everything.* Sinful human nature takes us to some strange places doctrinally, theologically, and personally; knowing our history is an important part of guarding against the mistakes of the past and making new ones in the future."

Seven reasons it is crucial to preserve local church history:

1. To obey Scripture's command to remember.
2. To preserve the accurate account of your local church for future generations.
3. To introduce your congregation to their identity in the denomination and church-at-large.
4. To create corporate memories to inspire and motivate current and future congregations.
5. To establish legal precedent and record.
6. To add to the greater Free Will Baptist history.
7. To satisfy your own curiosity about your heritage.

A BRIDGE TO THE FUTURE

On March 9, 1994, as a senior undergraduate student at Welch College, I sat transfixed as Jack Williams shared the story of the 1911 merger between New England Freewill Baptists and Northern Baptists. His presentation, appropriately titled "The Day We Lost Six Hundred Churches," traced the unfortunate series of events that contributed to this denominational disaster: the loss of theological distinctives and the subtle encroachment of ecumenism to unethical "back-door deals" between denominational officials on both sides of the merger.

However, his concluding remarks[5] impacted me most that day. Williams told spellbound listeners:

> *"There will never be another merger like 1911, if we preach Free Will Baptist distinctives, if we make a conscious effort to preserve and promote our Free Will Baptist name, and if we teach the next generation our history and heritage."*
> ***—Jack Williams***

That was the moment Free Will Baptist history captured my heart. From that day, I made it my goal to do my part to tell the incredible story of what God has done in and through Free Will Baptists, to help others retain, research, and write their own stories about their part in God's plan to work through His people.

CHAPTER TWO

BEFORE YOU START

It seemed good to me also...(Luke 1:3).

Having observed the importance of recording local church history, the prospective historian can turn attention to the *process* of creating that story. Any history project will flow more smoothly when it follows a plan. This chapter helps the writer consider five simple yet important questions that should be answered before starting the project: who, what, when, how, and how much.

WHO?

Who will lead this effort? Often, local church history results from the interest of an individual who becomes both catalyst and conscience for the completion of the project. That does not mean the individual must work alone. For some churches, a team approach works best, whether a group of casual "history buffs" or an official committee selected and approved by the church. Whatever the case, Robert E. Picirilli acknowledges the project benefits from the leadership of a particular type of individual: "If a church wants a written history, it would be well-served to find someone with a deep interest in history and the ability to write. Then involve a wide range of people in editing, correcting, and reviewing the work."

Donald Hughes agrees that a single person may guide the creation of a local church history but also warns the task is no job for a "Lone Ranger." He encourages developing a support team.[6] Why embrace the team approach? First, compiling a local church history is not easy; it involves a great deal of time and effort. Second, a team has a greater chance of locating, analyzing, and organizing historical resources. Finally, the project as a whole will benefit from the involvement of a greater number of people. Excitement rises, word of the historical project spreads, and the broader audience will—knowingly or unknowingly—help promote and publicize the finished work more effectively than any individual.

WHAT, WHEN, AND HOW?

Whether working alone or as a team, Donald Hughes encourages the prospective author(s) to gain support of the pastor and church leaders with a "well-reasoned and orderly" proposal.[7] The proposal should answer important questions:

What will the project include? Define the finished product carefully. For some churches, a simple booklet may be enough. For other congregations, the project may include a book, pictorial history, electronic publishing, and more. The scope of the work will vary by the church and its particular needs. Establish what fits the congregation best and spell it out in detail. While this volume focuses primarily on producing a book, it offers guidelines that may prove helpful for producing other formats.

Possible project formats:

- Pamphlet-styled book (5.5 inches by 8.5 inches) ranging from 32-48 pages.
- Full-length book. Soft or hardcover; length and size determined by the author or church.
- Pictorial or annotated pictorial history of the church.
- Electronic publishing (e-Pub), PDF document, third-party digital platform, or web.
- Multi-week church bulletin inserts or audio-visual presentations during church services.

When will the project be published? Often, local church histories are published in conjunction with a major anniversary or landmark achievement, such as the dedication of a new build-

> Whatever time you think it will take to complete your history, add six months... at least.
> —Phillip Morgan

ing. During the months and years leading up to such occasions, the congregation develops a natural curiosity about its history, and widespread support (and funding) are easier to obtain.

Whether the project marks a special occasion or not, it is crucial to set an expected completion date and allow sufficient time. A short church history may require six to eight months, while a full-length book may require eighteen months to two years (or more) to complete.

Phillip Morgan warns against the greatest threat to any local church history: insufficient time. He notes it takes far more time than anyone would dream. He advises, "Whatever time you think it will take to complete your history, add six months...at least." Morgan also lists a number of potential "historical hazards" that can delay or even derail a project entirely: missing (or nonexistent) records, conflicting accounts, production delays, and any of a multitude of distractions.

How will the project be produced? What process will it follow? For the individual writer, this question proves less complicated. For a group, every member of the team should have a clear understanding of the editorial process from the outset. Consider the following questions: Will a single writer produce the historical content? Or will multiple writers contribute? Who will review and compile the text into a single document? Will a historical board or committee have editorial control, or even "veto power" when necessary? Who will make final decisions regarding potentially divisive stories that arise during research? Who will establish the look and feel of the design? What team member(s) will guide and approve design layout and packaging?

Addressing these questions and others like them *before* the project begins will prevent hurt feelings, reduce tension, and lead to a smoother production process.

Another important consideration is the *historical approach* taken by the project, the perspective from which it is written. Will it be a *chronological narrative*, the story of the church as it unfolded in linear progression? Chronology gives readers the complete "bird's eye" overview of history but leaves little room for the details, minutia, and anecdotes many readers crave.

Perhaps your church history will take a *character-based* approach, tracing the lives of significant individuals in the life of the church. Character studies work especially well for churches with limited historical documentation. They give the writer an opportunity to take a "deep dive" into specific characters, sharing fascinating details and bringing characters to life.

A church with a deep collection of historical documents may rely heavily on those records, reproducing them as *autographs* and stringing them together with captions or paragraphs to create a visually-stunning, documentary-styled historical record.

Other historical approaches include highlighting *significant church milestones* or creating a *pictorial history*.

Local church history can be produced in various valid forms. The writer or team must decide the approach that best fits the available documentation and personality of the church. Refer to *Appendix D* for examples.

Historical Approaches

Chronological narratives tell the story of the church from beginning to end.

Character studies trace the lives and achievements of significant individuals in the life of the church.

Reproductions of records or significant historical documents (autographs) with captions piece together a historical mosaic of the church.

Milestones touch on significant dates and accomplishments in the history of the church.

Pictorial histories capture the life of the church in images.

HOW MUCH?

How much will the project cost, and how will the church or individual writer fund it? While every local church history budget is different based on the length, depth, and complexity of the project, Michael Lytle suggests three areas the individual or committee must consider:

Writing. If the church cannot produce its own historical text, it must hire a writer. This endeavor can become expensive, with freelance rates increasing more every year. When choosing a freelance writer, Lytle encourages a *full-project bid*—a single price for writing the entire book—rather than an hourly bid. This full-project price will help the church avoid ballooning costs if writing requires more time than expected.

Even when the writer comes from within the church family, expenses will be incurred for research and writing: copies, transcript fees, travel, the purchase of historical books and materials, and (depending on the project) photo restoration. Additionally, with the amount of time and effort involved in writing a local church history, if the responsibility falls on a single individual, a healthy honorarium is appropriate.

Design. Once the text is in hand, someone must reformat the text and accompanying photos or graphics into book form. Lytle encourages churches not to cut corners in this area, settling for poor layout when they have an important story to tell. "After all the time and effort (and money) invested in research and writing, don't hand out dog-eared photocopies stapled at the corners. Instead, spend the money to design a book of which the church can be proud."

Don't hand out dog-eared photocopies stapled at the corners. Instead, spend the money to design a book of which the church can be proud.
—Michael Lytle

This investment into quality design and production will be paid back in congregational satisfaction and increased sales. (For more on sales and promotion, refer to chapter seven.)

Two types of design must be considered: cover design and interior design. While both are important, remember the cover will help sell the books. Be willing to pay a professional for cover design, despite the cost. When it comes to interior page design, quality layout software is preferred (and sometimes required) by printers, whether Adobe InDesign or Quark Xpress. Avoid designing in Word, Docs, or other word processing software. These products, though useful for writers and office teams, are not intended for page design, and can create a nightmare for the printer who receives the files.

When using a freelance designer or design firm, plan to pay one price for standard, text-page design and another, higher price for design-heavy pages (those containing photographs, charts, or tables).

Printing. Before seeking a printing bid, determine several things about the project. What type of book will it be? Softcover, hardback, spiral bound, or coffee table quality? What length will it be? Before contacting printers, prepare the following information: page count (roughly), trim size (book dimensions), desired completion date, and binding.

This information is necessary because, when you request a bid, you seek a simple, per-book cost to help formulate your proposal. However, the printer must consider many variables when returning a bid: condition of the layout; cost of pre-press (processing the book files); the type of press needed for printing; cutting, folding, collating; paper quality; hand finishing, and so on. For this reason, Lytle warns it is difficult to provide a general or "rule of thumb" estimate for printing costs. Yet, he offers the following general guide for pricing.

Information for printing bids:

- Type of book? Hardback, softcover, spiral bound, coffee table, etc.
- Length (how many pages)?
- Trim size (dimensions)?
- Date needed?
- Color or black and white?
- Type of paper?

When printing 150 softcover, 32-page, staple-bound books (a standard church history booklet), the church will pay roughly $2.50 per book for printing and binding. Lytle identifies several common upgrades that increase the price dramatically: color printing, high-end paper, and a complex cover or binding.

When asked if a short turnaround time increases printing costs, Lytle quips, "It should!" But then, he admits with a smile that if a church is not printing thousands of copies of a lengthy book, most presses can turn around a small job quickly without raising the cost. The important thing is to be clear about the deadline up front and then to hit that deadline to avoid putting unexpected pressure on the printer. Churches can plan sixty to ninety days as the standard time for printing and binding.

Lytle encourages churches to request three print bids to develop an accurate financial picture for the project. "Be sure to include Randall House & D6 Family Ministry," he urges. "Not only because we do the work, but because we also share the values of your Free Will Baptist church. This is not true of every printer, and I think it is definitely worth something."

For more information on printing, contact Randall House & D6 Family Ministry at 800-877-7030. After receiving the general specifications above, Randall House & D6 Family Ministry typically returns a bid within a week.

With the cost of writing, designing, and printing in hand, combine the information into a simple-to-read summary and present it to church leaders, along with ideas for funding and promoting the project. "Then give leadership room to make the final decision," Lytle advises. "Get things 85-90% there on your proposal then hand it over to them for final adjustments. Understand church leadership may not be willing to make the same investment you are, so be ready to live with their decision. Find a way to 'make it happen' within their parameters."

FINAL THOUGHTS

After answering these important questions—*why, who, what, when, how,* and *how much*—and after seeking and gaining the support of the church, you (or your team) are almost ready to begin researching and writing. Phillip Morgan, who recently completed writing the two hundred-year history of a Middle Tennessee church, offers three suggestions based on

Before you go any further, make up your mind that history, and especially church history, must be *dedicated* to the pursuit of truth. —Phillip Morgan

his own experiences. First, he urges writers not to "cheat" the planning stage, admitting with a wry smile, "If I had it to do over, before I ever started writing, I would plan more...*much* more."

Second, he urges the writer or team to read *Free Will Baptists in History* by William Davidson, Michael Pelt's *A History of the Original Free Will Baptists, The Free Will Baptist Handbook* by J. Matthew Pinson, and the *Free Will Baptist Treatise.* These books provide a broad overview and framework of the entire history and doctrine of Free Will Baptists. It is especially important to understand how your church relates to the larger denominational picture, Morgan explains, because the church "did not just 'spring up' by itself; it came from somewhere, and you need to trace those roots."

Finally, Morgan encourages writers to brace themselves for what lies ahead and to be willing to discover the accepted narrative may not be true. "When that time comes," he urges, "you must be brave enough to say that. Some people may not like what you say. For that matter, *you* may not like what the truth leads you to say. But before you go any further, make up your mind that history, and especially church history, must be *dedicated* to the pursuit of truth."

CHAPTER THREE

RECORDING AND PRESERVING CHURCH RECORDS

Which from the beginning were eyewitnesses...(Luke 1:2).

Careful creation and preservation of congregational records is an essential part of preserving local church history. According to Keith Burden, good recordkeeping has a strong biblical basis. He points to three Old Testament examples: the numbering of the Israelite army in preparation for military campaigns, the requirement for priests to trace their family lineage, and the Persian records that ultimately saved Mordecai's life in the book of Esther.[8]

While insistent accurate records are important, Burden also acknowledges, "Churches are notorious for being poor record keepers!"[9] As a result, many local church histories are lost to the passage of time and poor recordkeeping. With these things in mind, how can a church effectively preserve good records?

Biblical Examples of Records

1. The Lord orders a numbering of Israel's army before military campaigns (Numbers 1:3; 26:35).
2. Priests are disqualified from carrying out their duties due to insufficient recordkeeping (Ezra 2:59, 62).
3. The life of Mordecai, Esther's cousin, is spared as a result of careful recordkeeping (Esther 2:23; 6:1–10).

FIND A SYSTEM

Establish a system for keeping records and follow that system. Burden urges churches to establish guidelines that meet the approval of the pastor and church leaders and to be consistent in adhering to those guidelines. He observes, "There is not necessarily a right way or wrong way to keep records, but they *must* be kept consistently."

Robert Picirilli advises the system should be established by the church rather than the current clerk, thus compelling each subsequent clerk to follow the desires of the church. Once a system of recordkeeping has been established, the church should write and record a simple policy within official church documents to avoid any confusion about the wishes of the church about recordkeeping.

What should church records include? Picirilli offers a simple, one-sentence formula: "Obviously, include the minutes, and then include anything that helps clarify those minutes—committee reports, treasurer's reports—anything not included in the minutes themselves."

Burden goes into greater detail, suggesting four broad areas for recordkeeping. First, he advises churches to keep up-to-date membership records. "Far too many churches wait years to update their records about deaths, births, and lost or gained members," Burden notes. Without a clear membership record, it is difficult for churches to establish accurate voting blocks.

Second, keep careful records of business meetings and proceedings—church minutes. When the church makes a change in policy or another important decision, that action requires something official, in writing, to show the action has been taken.

Third, record financial information. While the church treasurer is usually charged with bookkeeping, a chronological collection of financial reports included in (or accompanying) church minutes will prove beneficial to future church leaders and historical researchers by providing a clear picture of the financial health of the church.

Finally, Burden encourages good statistical records (attendance, births, deaths, and marriages) to document the growth and decline of the church family throughout time.

Suggested Content for Minutes

- Date and type of meeting (regular, called, annual, etc.)
- Start time and finish time
- Official actions and decisions
- Motions and resolutions, including who made and seconded each motion
- Treasurer's reports or additional financial reports
- Committee reports
- Significant staff actions (hiring, resignation, etc.)
- Membership decisions

COMPOSING MINUTES

The content of church minutes varies by church according to the bylaws and requirements of leadership. In the most basic form, church minutes should record all official actions and decisions taken by the church. Carol Pipes identifies two approaches to recording minutes. The first creates detailed minutes of the meeting; the second provides a brief summary or overview. "For me," she observes, "the type of minutes I take depends on the organization, but I *prefer* an abbreviated summary—briefly recording specific actions taken by voting members of the body." The process of recording these actions can be simplified with the following suggestions:

Make it easy. Picirilli advises the clerk to make sure minutes are dated, readable, identified well, and easily accessible. He shares, "I can't tell you how often church minutes start with no date, time, or occasion—just 'The church met Sunday night....'" To avoid this confusion, carefully identify the date of the meeting, the type or purpose of the meeting, the number of eligible voters attending, and the time the meeting begins and ends. Matt Pinson suggests clerks carefully record events of the meeting by noting who made each motion and second, and by putting as much information about each motion as space allows.

Keep it brief. Burden encourages church clerks to follow Jack Williams' rule for writing: *say it in the fewest words possible.* Pipes agrees: "I don't think you have to capture every word spoken. Try to capture major points and themes. Serve as a reporter. Describe a brief snapshot of what happens in the meeting."

In this quest for brevity, remember it is not necessary to record discussion about decisions, but simply to record specific actions taken by the church. Trying to summarize discussion tempts the clerk to insert his or her own view about the decision, when the clerk's job is simply to record facts, not to comment on those facts. "I avoid editorializing in minutes," concludes Carol Pipes. "It is fine to summarize, but it is *not* the job of the clerk to editorialize. Record the decision—and yes—

describe the response to the decision. Just avoid inserting *your* opinion regarding the decisions." While some churches do not record motions or resolutions that do not pass, at times failed motions and resolutions are helpful when piecing together the history and personality of a congregation.

Pipes identifies another important area that should not be overlooked in minutes: the spiritual side. "I always include the spiritual side of the meeting: when someone opens in prayer, leads a devotion, or shares pertinent Scripture. It is important to record these moments, both for our story and also for legal reasons as we link our spiritual side to our church polity. It is always wonderful to look back at previous generations and see the Word of God as the single thread running throughout our history that ties the organization together."

Keep it consistent. Find a simple formula or structure for writing minutes and stick to it. Over time, this consistent style will streamline minutes and make it easier for future clerks, church leaders, or historians to locate needed information quickly. Though the contents of minutes vary by church, Burden suggests the following structure for each action: Motion to... Seconded by...Motion passed. Others reduce this even further—and perhaps too far—by using MSC (a widely-used acronym for Motion, Seconded, and Carried), which omits the names of those making the motion and second and reports only on the motion itself. Be careful not to omit important facts. Any reporting structure chosen should adopt the goal of providing maximum historical data in the briefest form possible.

Make it yours. Obviously, the church cannot keep everything. Many pastors and church leaders become frustrated with rows of filing cabinets filling the church office and overflowing with everything from local newspapers to denominational brochures or pamphlets. A good rule of thumb to keep the church office from looking as though it is run by hoarders is to keep only those items produced by (or about) the church. Trust district, state, and denominational archives to preserve broader associational literature. Rely upon the local newspaper office to archive their back issues. Don't feel it necessary to house the history of every church or organization—just yours.

Keep it together. While an advocate of brief minutes, Burden warns church clerks not to sacrifice important historical data for the sake of brevity. He urges clerks to include the full text of resolutions, motions, and official decisions. When a decision or resolution is listed in the minutes without the accompanying details—the full text of the item—the information often will be lost to history.

Pinson agrees, noting, "Too often, you find church minutes with a reference to some action taken by the church but no record of the action itself, or what it entailed. 'Motion, second, and carried' is a great place to start, but more information is needed. It is crucial not to let important church decisions be lost to history."

"When a committee brings a recommendation to the body," adds Pipes, "they usually create handouts. It is helpful to keep these documents with the minutes and refer to them by name (Recommendation 1, Resolution 1, or some other designation), so researchers can match the resolution, recommendation, or motion with the appropriate accompanying document."

Pinson suggests the church clerk compile an annual notebook of church minutes that includes a heavy-duty cellophane sleeve or envelope. Throughout the year, the clerk should accumulate any item that might explain the minutes to readers in a careful, chronological order. "Low tech is not a bad thing," Pinson advises. "These days, we tend to dismiss anything not done on a computer, but paper and plastic are your friends when it comes to preserving records." Well-organized notebooks, with clear labeling of the notebooks as an official supplement to the church minutes, make it harder to discard these important records. This is good, Pinson concludes, because simple files are too easy to discard.

Ask *who* and *why*, not just *what* and *when*. Pinson encourages clerks to keep bulletins, notes from committee meetings or deacons' meetings, reports from committees to the church, building proposals, and so forth. Why is it important to collect this supporting material for church minutes? Why are these types of records important to preserve? "Because these items tell *why* it happened, not just *what* and *when* it happened," answers Pinson. "*What* and *when* is the goal of church minutes, but when your records answer *who* and *why* in addition to *what* and *when*, you help future generations capture a greater overall picture of your congregation."

> These items tell *why* it happened, not just *where* and *when* it happened.
> —Matt Pinson

Consider two final pieces of advice regarding the creation of minutes. First, record them promptly. Burden urges clerks not to procrastinate when writing the minutes, but to record them immediately. He recalls a statement made by his junior high algebra teacher, who told the class, "A short pencil is better than a long memory."

Don't wait to complete the minutes. Record details immediately while they are still fresh on your mind. Pipes adds another simple tip for accurate reporting: "I always record meetings on my phone, so I can go back and listen to areas that were unclear."

Finally, Burden urges clerks to take their jobs seriously. "In far too many cases," he notes, "church clerks only serve because no one else will take the job. But the clerk is essential to the ministry of the church, both now and for the future. Just filling the position is not enough. Give it your all."

FIND A PLACE

One of the basic responsibilities of the church clerk, Robert E. Picirilli notes, is to find a good place where records won't rot, become lost, or burn up. Burden encourages clerks to have "at least two places to store church records, one inside the church and one outside the church. This will prevent loss in case of fire or accidental discarding of these important files."

Use common sense. Far too many churches have lost the story of their congregation due to fire, flooding, or negligence. The following simple suggestions help secure records:

- Invest in locking, fire-safe, water-resistant filing systems.
- Use acid-free archive boxes and file folders to protect documents against deterioration.
- Store records off the ground to protect against minor flooding.

- Use climate-controlled storage to avoid fluctuations in temperature and humidity; invest in a good dehumidifier.
- While it is tempting to display early records for sentimental or historical reasons, avoid placing them in direct sunlight that might damage or destroy them over time.
- Never add moldy or mildewed records to a "dry" collection without treatment, because the rot will spread and destroy the entire collection.
- Organize and label carefully to avoid accidental loss.

Take advantage of new technology. Desktop computers and scanners make preserving church records much easier than it was for previous generations. Many of today's copiers and printers include a scanning feature. If your church copier does not have scanning technology, invest in a modestly priced flatbed scanner and make it a goal to scan and store everything electronically. If nothing else, digital apps turn any smartphone into an effective portable scanner.

While creating these digital copies of church records is important, Burden warns it is also important to retain records in physical form. "Protect the original copies," Burden advises, "and make provision for a backup in case of natural disaster or accidental loss."

Once digital copies of church records have been created, use available technology to organize and preserve the records. As with paper records, digital technology requires careful handling.

Make multiple copies. Follow the same guidelines for digital records you would for physical records. Keep a backup in the church library or archives and another offsite. Most church record archives fit easily on a USB hard drive (sometimes described as a *flash drive* or *thumb drive*). Flash drives are an inexpensive investment to ensure the safety of the church's digital collection. Currently, portable solid state hard drives (SSD) are the preferred standard for archiving digital records. Like flash technology, these drives have no moving parts to wear out. They are small (roughly the dimensions of a credit card and less than a quarter-inch thick), and relatively inexpensive. The church can purchase a high quality SSD with significant storage space without blowing the annual budget. Internet cloud storage provides another convenient option. Remember, the type of storage used is not as important as ensuring the collection is safely archived in multiple locations.

Keep digital storage updated. As time passes, technology evolves, and church archives may become inaccessible by new devices. Over the last three decades, floppy disks, zip drives, CD-ROMs, and most recently DVD-ROMs all had their day as the standard for digital storage. Today, all have been replaced by safer, faster, and more reliable technology. This reality underscores the importance of Burden's suggestion to keep at least one physical copy of church records.

Update and back up records annually. To avoid an insurmountable backlog of files, set aside a specific time each year to scan, organize, and add records to your archive. This annual deposit provides a natural time to back up the collection or check on upgrading technology. Think of it as a necessary seasonal activity similar to changing out batteries in smoke detectors.

Burden offers one final piece of advice to new church clerks: "Find the best church clerk you can, sit down for a conversation,

Few things are more valuable to local church history than a *conscientious and organized clerk.* —Keith Burden

observe the system used, and then follow that example."

Burden recalls years of serving as assistant to Waldo Young, long-time clerk of the National Association of Free Will Baptists. "I remember being amazed at his wisdom and insight. He was usually spot-on when predicting the outcomes of business decisions. Although he seldom spoke or expressed opinions publicly, I had the chance to hear some of the things he said under his breath at the clerk's table. I still chuckle over some of them."[10]

More importantly, Burden notes that Young was never too busy to explain things to his young, inexperienced assistant eager to learn. He was not possessive or territorial. "And, when he finally stepped down after 30 years of service, he graciously handed over the reins and walked away. I will always appreciate his commitment and loyalty to our denomination."[11]

Burden's words are a good reminder that few things are more valuable to local church history, and ultimately denominational history, than a conscientious and organized clerk.

If you are a new clerk, make up your mind to do your best to preserve church history. If you have been a faithful church clerk for decades, thank you. Please find someone to mentor. Share the tips and tricks you have learned, and instill the importance of good recordkeeping in the next generation.

CHAPTER FOUR

READY FOR RESEARCH

Having had perfect understanding of all things...(Luke 1:3).

"Research is the cornerstone of a successful local church history,"[12] writes Donald Hughes. His claim is true. The success of any history project rises or falls on the quality of research done by the author or team. "Research is to writing what taking an oath is to a witness in court," Jack Williams observed. "It gives your work the credibility readers are seeking."[13]

Research is systematic investigation that gathers knowledge or data from primary sources and firsthand accounts. Research can be divided into two types or categories: acquisition and assimilation.

Acquisition involves locating and obtaining the sources of data: previous histories, church archives, interviews with long-time members (or previous historians), community records, denominational resources, and web resources.[14] *Assimilation* describes the process of reviewing, verifying, and sorting the accumulated data into the narrative being created.

Research must be logical, objective, even ruthless in verifying the data collected, Williams advised.[15] He encouraged writers to document relentlessly. "Just putting something into print does not make it true," he warned. "If someone wants to follow up your facts, they need to know where to go to do so. The cardinal rule for research and writing: if you can't prove it, don't print it!"[16]

What is the ultimate goal of research? Research provides the context for the story of your congregation. Robert Morgan observes, "Context is critical because we are living in a time without context." He recalls family trips of previous decades when mom or dad would stop by the local gas station and buy a map to see the big picture. The family would gather around the dining room table to plan out a route, considering the geography and attractions along the way.

He warns, "Today, all we see is a tiny screen on our dashboard, with a detached voice telling us 'turn left here.' Younger generations, especially, live in a world without context, where context is no longer important—but it is."

Good research provides the context, the big picture. It gives the writer a backdrop against which to craft a story that will meet the current generation's hunger for belonging and help them understand the larger picture of their church, their family, and most importantly, their faith.

THE "SHORTCUT" TO WRITING

While the next chapter is dedicated to the writing process, a simple "shortcut" throughout the research phase will prove invaluable once writing starts. What is this shortcut? ***Create detailed written notes regarding your research.*** Phillip Morgan encourages researchers to take notes, make copies, organize information, and pull out any facts important for the greater project. Keith Burden suggests compiling a simple list of categories to be covered by the project and inserting careful notes from research into each appropriate matching category.

"Write as you go," advises Matt Pinson. "I keep notes on my computer as I research, and by the time I finish the research stage, often the whole article, essay, or book can simply be lifted from my notes. When I am ready to write, it is just a matter of copy and paste, lifting text from my notes and placing the information where it belongs in the greater story."

RESEARCH IN SIX STEPS...PLUS ONE

While every historian develops his or her own unique approach to research, in nearly every case, that process includes the following six steps: 1) locate previous histories; 2) find, organize, and review church minutes; 3) search the church for hidden gems; 4) conduct interviews; 5) consult associational minutes; and 6) search local newspaper archives and county clerk's office.

Before you dive into research, take some advice from Jack Williams: "When it comes to research, let common sense guide you. Nose around where instincts lead. Don't fear unorthodox sources; seek the obscure, yet don't overlook the obvious."[17]

Locate previous histories. "Find out who has done previous research, and you will save countless hours of time and effort,"[18] Williams advised. Phillip Morgan agrees, noting that even when writers do not use all the information obtained from previous histories, the information helps the individual or team gain a broader understanding of the church's overall history.

Robert Picirilli describes this step as the pursuit of the big picture: "I try to get an overall 'big picture' of what I am dealing with before I ever start writing," he confides. "If it is an area where I don't have a big picture, I take a whole lot of notes from various sources."

"I read and read," concurs Carol Pipes. "I put my hands on *everything* that has already been written—articles, books, interviews, reports. I may not read every word, but I skim it all, trying to gain as much information and background as possible."

Where can these previous publications be found? Start in the church office or library. If that search proves fruitless, appeal to the congregation. Often, church history books or pamphlets have graced coffee tables and bookshelves in congregational homes for decades (or perhaps found their way into the back of the hall closet). Church members, especially aging members, are usually eager to share their keepsakes to assist in producing the next chapter in the church's history.

If an exhaustive search of church and congregation reveals little, visit Welch Library's online catalog, enter the church name, and see what appears. Don't be discouraged if you don't get results, advises Phillip Morgan. "The church name may have been changed or abbreviated. Expand your search and abbreviate the name or previous names." If you locate material about your church in the collection, stop by or contact the staff for help in obtaining the information. Morgan offers one other warning about searching for church history. If your church has a common name, be sure you find the *right* church history. Otherwise, you could inadvertently produce a wonderful church history project for another congregation.

Mary Ruth Wisehart believed this search for books or documents is well worth the time and effort. While writing her doctoral dissertation, she learned the only existing copy of a rare book she needed was housed in the Smithsonian. She appealed to Washington and was granted hands-on access. "Without that particular volume, I would have been unable to complete my work," she recalled. "It was a great deal of effort to locate and obtain this source, but it was the turning point in my research."

Find, organize, and review church minutes. Once previous histories have been located and reviewed, turn attention to the minutes of the church and accompanying records, the primary source of information for church researchers.[19]

Unfortunately, not every church—especially those existing for more than a century—has a complete run of minutes. Many churches did not record minutes, and others lost records to leadership changes, over-zealous purging, fire, or some other natural disaster. Once again, the researcher may need to scour the church office, library, and closets and appeal to the congregation to locate all existing copies.

Once every source has been exhausted, the researcher should organize minutes into chronological order and review from beginning to end (taking notes along the way). This sequence will help researchers capture Picirilli's "big picture" of the church.

Phillip Morgan notes with a chuckle, "Yes, it is important to read your church minutes...*if* you can find them, and *if* you can stand reading them." Reading church minutes can be dry and tedious, yet this discipline is crucial for research. Morgan encourages researchers to remember that historical research is often like detective work. "As you struggle through the minutes, keep in mind you are looking for the one 'clue' that may unlock the deepest mysteries of your church." This sleuthing mindset makes perusing minutes more enjoyable.

Throughout the search, Picirilli advises researchers to "follow the clues from those familiar journalistic questions *who, what, when, why,* and *where,* asking 'What happened?' 'Who did it?' and 'When was it?'"

Consider three important guidelines as you prepare to review minutes:

1. Be thorough. After countless hours of poring over records that read remarkably like the ones before, it can be tempting to skip important sections. Don't get bogged down in the endless stream of motions. Learn to focus on identifying things that have made your church what it is today. Wisehart encouraged, "As you read, ask, 'What are the most important things to the history of this church?' and you may be surprised to find one special moment that ties everything else together."

Make notes about anything that altered the course of the church's history. Don't be afraid of taking too many notes. As the focus of research narrows, particular themes, milestones, and characters will emerge as the "backbone" of the project. It is far easier to write with too much information than too little.

2. Be impartial. Researchers are likely to discover surprising and sometimes troubling facts about the church. Avoid the urge to rewrite history, or to paint individuals or decisions in a better light. Record quotes carefully and summarize accurately in your notes. "Always be impartial," Jack Williams warned. "Avoid prejudice. Partiality in print so deeply offends people that you are not likely to be forgiven in this life...or the life to come if readers have anything to say about it." "Don't be biased," concluded Wisehart. "That is the most important piece of advice I can offer any researcher."

3. Be objective. Arthur Walker advises the cardinal principle of all historical interpretation is "to avoid reading into a statement or action a meaning it did not convey originally. A misrepresentation is not an interpretation."[20]

Walker advises three steps to help the researcher avoid misinterpreting records: 1) define obsolete or vernacular terms to avoid misunderstanding; 2) identify the bias and, at times, the competence level of the minutes writer; and 3) verify church records through other historical accounts, denominational records, and secular records (newspapers, public information).[21] "Be open-minded," advises Picirilli. "Don't make up your mind about what you will find before you start your research."

Search the church for "hidden gems." Phillip Morgan encourages researchers to make the extra effort of organizing a "scavenger hunt" through the oldest, deepest closets in the church to discover the hidden gems they contain. Why is this step important? No one wants to read restated church minutes. "You can add some 'meat to the bones' you have put together through unofficial records," says Morgan. Search for church programs, missionary programs, ordination services, weddings, special events in the life of the church, or even an old photograph that will tell the story far more effectively than you ever could. Morgan encourages researchers to extend a general call to any church member who might own historical materials, and to be ready to wade through the stacks of materials received. "You may not find much," Morgan observes, "but you never know when you will uncover the hidden treasure that will change the direction of your work."

Pinson describes these materials (formally termed *realia* or *ephemera*) as "shoebox history." He puts together all this type of material he can find, sifting through it to piece things together. While Pinson begins research with interviews and minutes, he notes the importance of reviewing *any* material that further reveals the character—and characters—of the church. "I look at flyers, bulletins, Sunday School campaigns, revival records, and more," Pinson shares. "These items offer a personal history, a flair to the stark data in the minutes."

Conduct interviews. Pinson advises researchers to begin with interviews when writing the history of any church 75 years old or younger. "I always start my research with oral histories, especially if charter members are still living," he notes. "These interviews add a personal touch to the history of your church." Carol Pipes agrees, noting she relies heavily on oral interviews, both first person and with experts familiar with the church to add great "color" to the story. Sometimes, the most significant results of one interview are discovering the questions to ask in the next.

While Picirilli acknowledges any writer compiling a local church history must interview longstanding members of the congregation, he cautions: "Historians must keep in mind that interviews are subjective and may contain faulty memories. Facts gleaned in interviews should be verified where possible and qualified when they cannot be verified."

Though Wisehart encouraged interviewers to enjoy interesting people and their interesting stories, she also advised researchers to be prepared to verify. "Some people won't even accept oral interviews as valid research," she warned. "But I've learned you can't believe everything in print, either. Start with older members of the congregation. Listen to their stories and then verify through church records."

Phillip Morgan doesn't place as high a value on interviews as some church historians. Still, like Wisehart, he acknowledges their value, especially as it relates to providing insight to church records. He advises, "Find the oldest living members of your church and glean all you can from their memories."

He warns researchers that interviews will require them to return to the minutes or previous histories to verify information or to read more about previously overlooked items. Morgan also warns against the dangers of misleading or even disingenuous interviews: "Memories are skewed; people unintentionally, and sometimes intentionally, alter the truth to rewrite the history of church or family."

CONDUCTING EFFECTIVE INTERVIEWS

Researchers should follow four steps for effective and productive interviews:

Prepare well. Robert Morgan identifies two sides to a good interview. "The first is simply being prepared, knowing what you are going to ask the person, and what information you need to know. The other side is simply to enjoy the conversation as if you were talking with a friend."

Effective interviews require careful preparation. Beforehand, write questions designed to produce specific answers about emerging storylines, themes, or characters. Learn everything you can about the individual to be interviewed (technically defined as the *narrator*) and make appropriate notes. Set a time and place where both parties will be comfortable. When permission is granted, be prepared to record the interview. "Do your best to put people at ease," offered Wisehart. "Let them talk. Be willing to endure their stories. And, remember, if you don't want something to come out in print, don't put it down in print. Understand your notes from the interview will eventually cast that individual in a particular light. Be accurate yet kind."

Ask open-ended questions. A good interview is more than random reminiscing (though it should feel that way to the narrator). Ask open-ended, leading questions that require more than a simple yes or no answer. For instance, don't ask, "Were you at the church when Rev. Smith was the pastor?" Instead, ask, "*What do you remember* about Rev. Smith and his ministry at the church?"

Often, five carefully-prepared, open-ended questions will produce a lengthier, more productive interview than twenty poor questions. Don't be afraid to ask follow-up questions if the initial query fails to produce the desired information. A word of warning: if particular questions venture into controversial territory, start with "safe" questions first, or the interview may come to an abrupt end. Save "bombshell" questions for the final minutes of the interview and then preface them carefully: "I understand the next question may be difficult...." In these moments, a "soft question" will turn away wrath and perhaps keep the interview moving toward its expected conclusion.

Stay on track (unless you take a detour). While an interview should remain conversational and comfortable, from time to time, it may be necessary for the interviewer to return to key questions or themes if the narrator gets bogged down in minute details or personal opinion. Casual statements such as "Can we go back to something you said earlier?" or "May I follow up on something?" effectively steer the conversation back to the essential information to be gleaned.

Good interviewers must understand the delicate balance between pre-written questions and "hot leads" that may arise unexpectedly. Robert Morgan points to a careful balance between preparation and spontaneity, noting, "Some of the best interviews are those where you hear spontaneous stories. Be ready to go down a route you didn't expect to uncover a story you didn't know existed." Pursue "colorful" details that help the reader visualize the scene and bring the story to life.

Sometimes, a startling storyline emerges from an interview so powerful it overrules all other questions. Some years ago, during an interview with an elderly pastor and World War II veteran regarding his post-war ministry, he casually mentioned his service as a radio operator aboard the *U.S.S. Enterprise* aircraft carrier on the morning of the attack on Pearl Harbor. In light of the incredible events of that day, his offhand comment caught my attention. Before the interview concluded, I uncovered the remarkable story of the young man who transmitted that infamous radio message to a shocked world: "Japanese planes attacking Pearl Harbor—this is not a drill!" While the resulting article still featured the pastor's post-war ministry in Hawaii, it set his story against the backdrop of his role in one of the most significant moments in American history.

Don't wait. Sadly, not long after the interview with the pastor and veteran described above, he slipped quietly into eternity. Without his casual comment during the interview, readers would have missed a remarkable element of his life. Too many elderly church members pass from this life without sharing their stories. Don't delay in preserving their irreplaceable memories.

Remember one final resource for discovering and recording the oral history of the church: sermons. Whether written or recorded, sermons are an often overlooked yet valuable source of oral history, especially when delivered on special days or significant anniversaries. On these days, speakers often share anecdotal stories or accounts of church life that reveal valuable historical data.

Consult associational minutes. Missing segments of church history sometimes can be pieced together using the records of the district or quarterly association. Consult the local church clerk, who perhaps can provide contact information for an associational clerk. If your regional association doesn't archive minutes, check with long-time members of the association or visit www.FWBHistory.com to explore the largest repository of Free Will Baptist associational, state, and national minutes.

Ten Suggestions for Good Interviews

1. Prepare well.
2. Interview the subject (narrator) when he or she feels like talking (especially true for older church members).
3. Record the interview if permission is granted, but don't allow recording to be intrusive.
4. Pre-write the introduction and personal data.
5. Make the interview comfortable.
6. Ask open-ended, conversational questions leading to other questions.
7. Ask "safe" questions before pursuing controversial areas.
8. Ask for physical descriptions of pastors, church leaders, and other "notorious" members of the congregation to add spice and humor.
9. Stay on topic.
10. Be prepared to verify all facts.[22]

Search local newspaper archives and county clerk's office. "After the interviews and minutes have been completed, look to the newspapers," urged Wisehart. Phillip Morgan agrees, noting local newspapers are a great place to find articles or news items regarding the church, especially momentous occasions such as building dedications, ground breaking, or tragedies. Baptist historian Quentin Porch recalls that "in the early years of our country, most small towns had a local newspaper.... In many cases, the newspapermen were members of the local church.... Many ran announcements of the Sunday services and were delighted with any special occasion that gave them newsworthy material."[23]

While newspapers are a valuable source of information, Porch also identifies several challenges in newspaper research: lack of availability and accessibility; time required for the search; poor archival quality; and lack of accuracy. He encourages researchers to shorten their search for elusive newspaper nuggets by identifying the date, event, and subject before starting.[24] Today, newspaper archives often can be accessed online or in microform at local paper offices.

Wisehart pointed out the value of exploring historical Free Will Baptist congregational, regional, and state papers: "Don't just turn to secular papers, but remember Free Will Baptist papers such as the *Gem*, the *Free Will Baptist, The Morning Star,* and the *Echo.*" Many periodicals (dating to the early 1800s) are available for browsing or download at www.FWBHistory.com.

Public records in the county clerk's office or in the office of the register of deeds may provide hard-to-find information regarding church origins, rezoning, building permits, and more.

Sometimes, glaring discrepancies between original blueprints and existing structures prove both informative and humorous.

RESEARCH...PLUS ONE

While many researchers today turn to the Internet as their first stop for information, they may be surprised to discover little, if any, information regarding their local church. History must be written before it becomes available online.

Still, a number of web resources are useful for research. Genealogical sites provide scarce and valuable information about families in the congregation. You may be surprised to find church documents or a previously published history on Google Books, www.archive.org, or some other Internet archive. In short, as you begin the research phase, take time to do a quick Google search, but don't be dismayed if nothing about the church appears. After all, creating a local church history is your challenge and the reason for this book.

Robert E. Picirilli offers one final word of encouragement for researchers:

> *In gathering, organizing, and ultimately writing history, I have uncovered many interesting moments, and it seems providential. The truth is, I pray for the Lord to lead me to information that reveals those moments. Sometimes, a discovery He sends my way completely changes the direction of my writing. If you don't have the Lord's help, you probably won't find the things you need. Just keep hunting and hunting, and you will be amazed how you end up writing in a totally different area than intended.*

Tracing the Past: A Research Checklist

- Previous church histories
- Minutes and periodicals from the local church, along with quarterly, district, and state associations
- Pamphlets and books detailing the actions and events of denominational people and organizations
- Bulletins, flyers, photographs, posters, promotional materials, and other printed *realia* and *ephemera*
- Theological or doctrinal publications (treatises, statements of faith, and church covenants)
- Legal records
- Works by a pastor or church member
- Personal records and accounts: birth, marriage, and death records; diaries and journals; memoirs; unpublished biographies; and autobiographies
- Genealogical and web information

CHAPTER FIVE

A GUIDE TO (GOOD) WRITING

To write unto thee in order...(Luke 1:3).

Phillip Morgan quips, "You can't research forever. Eventually, you just need to stop and write." If research is the cornerstone of local church history, writing constructs the walls and

You can't research forever. Eventually, you just need to stop and write.
—Phillip Morgan

ceiling. Any thoughtful exploration of writing must consider two elements: the process of writing and the craft of writing. The *process* of writing considers the chronology of the project, concept to outline, and rough draft to completion. The *craft* of writing refers to the discipline, skill, and art of writing: grammar, sentence and paragraph structure, narrative flow, verb usage, and a myriad other important topics.

CAPTURING THE STORY

One important element, however, transcends every other aspect of writing: the *story*. Storytelling is vital to good communication. People long to be part of an unfolding narrative. Effective writers help readers understand their place in the history of the local church and in the redemptive plan of God. Robert Morgan describes stories as the "missing links" in most local church histories. "It is amazing how many writers leave out anecdotes," he observed. "They may write an *accurate* history, but without good stories, it is simply not an enjoyable one."

Carol Pipes urges writers to capture the story, not just to record details or report facts: "Find the story your readers won't be able to put down but will stay up all night to finish." Jack Williams observed, "When people read what you write, they are looking for three things: information, interpretation, and entertainment. Try to do all three in your writing, but if you can't, at least be entertaining. Tell the story."[25]

How does a writer identify a powerful story? Robert Morgan advises writers to get beyond the facts to find the *color*. "Share the accounts that make people readable, human, and touchable—not just factual statements—real flesh and blood struggles." Identifying key stories is not easy. Robert Morgan observes that too many writers and communicators go from project to print, speech, or sermon without the arduous, grinding process of mental meditation. "We express it without taking sufficient time, long walks to contemplate. We need to think it through, ponder it; take it for a walk on the beach or a hike in the mountains. This is just as important as filling the page. To find the right story, meditate on the facts and allow the idea to mature."

Pipes seeks out stories of conflict and resolution in the life of the church, times when the church faced and overcame challenges. "These stories of victory are engaging to readers because they understand them," she notes. "Every believer has experienced similar challenges, so connect readers to the conflict...and the resolution." Documentarian Victor Albright adds, "Find the thing that interests *you* and tell *that* story. Then consider the story from the perspective of others and answer the questions they have. That's the fundamental element of storytelling."

Robert E. Picirilli advises writers not to get bogged down in a restatement of church minutes but to write about things that "have made the church or association what it is today, things that altered the course of the church's history." Mary Ruth Wisehart described her process for identifying the story: "I look at all the gathered information and think, 'What are the most important things to the history of this church?' Then I find one special approach—one story, one theme—that ties everything together." Wisehart went on to note that after she captured her readers' attention, she kept their attention by building upon that unique storyline through the entire project.

Find the hero, advises Albright: "In a documentary, if you don't pick a protagonist and tell his or her story, no one will listen. You can list the facts—the situation, the dates and time—but if you don't tell the story of the hero, no one will listen."

"Identify the people and personalities, the movers and the shakers," concludes Matt Pinson. "Try to identify what made them do what they did. Anyone can create a chronology of *what* and *when.* But it is the *why*—the story behind the stories—that will capture readers."

THE PROCESS OF WRITING

Create an outline. A well-constructed outline is the *key* to writing history according to Donald Hughes, not only because it guides the flow of material and the narrative, but also because it makes the writer "less likely to let details fall through the cracks."[26] Hughes advises constructing a working outline *before* research begins. This initial outline will guide the research phase and funnel appropriate information toward the primary storyline and character development. Once the research phase has been completed, the outline can be refined based on research discoveries.[27]

Obviously, creating a preliminary outline requires some initial research and a clear vision for the approach the project will take: Picirilli's *big picture.* "Once I have an overall picture in mind, I simply start writing," Picirilli notes, "but I *begin* with an outline."

Pinson concurs: "I like to have an outline to guide the story—as detailed as I can get it!" According to Pinson, the outline should be based upon the particular approach to the story, whether chronological narrative, character vignettes, a particular theme, or a series of themes. "Once you determine the approach," he continues, "you determine the main things you want to cover."

For those concerned about "restricting" research by using an outline, Keith Burden offers helpful advice: "Label one category *miscellaneous* and use that category to record everything that defies categorization but is still important to the life and history of the church." "If you don't like the idea of an outline," Pinson offers, "don't call it an outline. Call it list of topics."

When creating the outline, Robert Morgan encourages writers to formulate the "unfolding logic" of what they want to say, the single point or theme that runs throughout the book. "There has to be an arrow through the heart of the whole thing—the theme, the thesis, what you want to say. But then, you want to 'notch' that arrow with unfolding points along the way, the logic of how you want to say it." Once the single point or theme is in place, Morgan creates a schema that lays the whole book out in a way that allows one section to build upon the next until "you have gone from 'the feather to the tip,' from introduction to conclusion. Then, it is just a matter of filling in the sentences and paragraphs to flesh out the rest of the book."

An Alternate Starting Point? Robert Morgan offers an alternative starting point to the writing process: the *introduction.* "I work really hard on the introduction. I may rewrite it fifty times...It sets the tone for the entire book, and it gives you a firm grasp on what you are ultimately saying. It shines a bright light on the rest of your pages."

Morgan compares a writer's planning and outlining process to Psalm 139:16, where the psalmist describes the divine plan for our lives written long before an individual's conception: "Thine eyes did see my substance, yet being unperfect; and *in thy book all my members were written,* which in continuance were fashioned, when as yet there was none of them." Morgan concludes, "Something about the unfolding logic and systematic creation of a book is very important."

Annotate the outline. Once the outline has been established, word-processing programs make it easy to list subjects or topics as subheads within the outline. Research discoveries can be organized and annotated where they fit.

By following this method, Pinson observes, "Soon, you see a book begin to take shape from the outline." He encourages writers not to wait until research has been completed to begin writing but to expand the outline into paragraph form throughout the research stage. "Sometimes, things come together so well in your research, that you *need to stop and write,* or you will lose a golden opportunity." In those moments, Pinson stops and writes immediately, noting that a fresh understanding of a subject or event is very helpful for writing.

Phillip Morgan encourages writers to take a similar approach for quoted material, both from print and oral sources. Put all interesting quotes down then arrange them chronologically or by theme under section headings. The writer can then copy and paste quotes into the expanding narrative where they fit best.

Put it all together. Phillip Morgan advises using three separate word-processing documents when writing. The first simply functions as a catchall where the writer records every fact discovered. The second is a working file where information is assimilated into an outline or list of topics. Finally, the two files are narrowed into a single document—the rough manuscript or narrative.

The initial manuscript may exceed, and perhaps far exceed, the planned length of the project, but not to worry. After proofing, rewriting, and correcting, the manuscript will be "whittled down to size," according to Picirilli. "No matter what I write, I overwrite," he confesses. "I produce too much. But then I pare it down and condense it. I write and write and rewrite, narrowing it to its final form."

COVERING DIFFICULT TOPICS

As the historical account takes shape, writers often deal with difficult, even divisive moments in the history of the local church. Three options exist for handling these topics: omit them, minimize or generalize them, or confront them.

To avoid "passing the buck" to the next generation, how *should* the writer handle difficult areas of church history? "Very carefully!" jokes Picirilli before offering four simple principles for exploring difficult storylines without splitting the church (or being removed from membership): *be objective, be honest, document relentlessly,* and *be kind.*

Be objective. The primary goal when dealing with difficult topics is objectivity. This doesn't mean a writer cannot insert his or her own opinion regarding a difficult period in the history of the church. It simply needs to be clear to readers he or she is doing so. "It's one thing to talk about *what* someone did," Picirilli concludes, "but it is another thing entirely to talk about *why* someone did it."

Mary Ruth Wisehart agreed, noting writers must remain as fair to both sides as possible, remaining objective even when it hurts. "Understand it is important for the two sides to learn about one another in a unifying way," she advised. "Not that they will ever agree, but to open dialogue about the subject."

Be honest. Double-check everything. Write only what you can prove, but don't back away from facts. If the facts are too painful or too personal to reveal in print, generalize rather than rewriting history or "sugar-coating" the truth about a difficult time or character. "When you write about historical figures, understand every person has skeletons in his closet," Ron Hunter advises. "Tip your hat to the skeletons; acknowledge they are there. But your church history should not read like a tabloid. No person or organization is perfect, only Christ."

Document relentlessly. Don't open the door to accusations of bias (or, worse yet, legal action) by writing facts that cannot be sourced. "You control the story until it goes to press," wrote Jack Williams. "But then it comes to life as either a vengeful Frankenstein or the U.S. Cavalry. Be very careful. Libel is the older brother of the vengeful Frankenstein in the preceding statement!"[28]

Document your research tirelessly, Williams advised, and write with the constant awareness that simply putting something into print does not make it true.

Be kind. Wisehart encouraged writers to understand difficult topics are very emotional to everyone involved. "At times, you need to have someone else read what you have written. He or she may identify sensitive areas to be changed or omitted completely."

Wisehart advised some things need to be written, but others should never be published because the information revealed is not worth the division created.

"We should not focus only on what went wrong in our history," Hunter adds, "but we should learn from people's mistakes, challenges, and shortcomings. Then highlight their strengths. Truly objective historians state the facts, acknowledge weaknesses but also demonstrate greatness to communicate a balanced view of the individual."

After reviewing one recent history project, Phillip Morgan acknowledges his determination to be kinder in the way he writes in the future, to avoid sentences and phrases that come across as sharp, and to eliminate unnecessary "shots" at other people and historians. Writing local church history is challenging, he explains, because "sometimes, you are writing about living people or their families, and it is very difficult to write painful truth. It's always easier to write about dead people, as calloused as that sounds."

In spite of the challenges of writing about difficult periods in the history of a church, Hughes urges writers to tell the *whole* story, even difficult or unpopular moments. "We do not want to skim over controversy. We do not want to hide bad things that happened. We do not want to falsify the facts. But we do want to glorify the Lord for the way He acted in the lives of individuals and in the congregation as a whole."[29]

THE CRAFT OF WRITING

The only way to become a good writer is by writing or reading good writing. Robert Morgan notes that writers who are readers have the ability to write words that "turn into pictures on the page. By changing just a word here or there, they bring a story to life."

Fourteen practical suggestions will benefit any writer:

Write to communicate, not to impress. Ditch big words. Lose complex storylines. Write what you mean and mean what you write. Writing is only as good as a reader's comprehension.

Start fast. Capture the attention of readers quickly, or you won't keep them at all. In this social-media driven world condensed to 280 characters, make contact immediately. Find your focus. Get to the point. Introduce the subject and storyline and repeat it often. Summarize succinctly.

Write lean. Use short words and eliminate unnecessary words. Don't say, "I remember when...." Just dive in. Use the fewest words possible to communicate clearly. Keep subjects and verbs together. Make sentences and paragraphs short. Save the strongest sentence for the end of the paragraph and the strongest word for the end of each sentence. Robert Morgan urges writers not to "make it as *concise* as possible but as *readable* as possible. You don't want unnecessary words; you don't want clutter."

Williams encouraged, "Don't tell me you can't shorten it. Let me remind you the greatest job of editing happened early one Sunday morning when four thousand years of history were condensed into seven words: 'He is not here; He is risen!'"[30]

Make verbs vital. Stop using passive verbs and lean on strong, descriptive, exciting verbs. Nix forms of "to be." Search for *be, is, are, am, was,* and *were* and replace them. Follow the old guideline that suggests strong verbs should comprise ten percent of your text.

Write like you speak. If you are not an experienced writer, simply write a picture. Visualize the story then describe it.

Learn everything you can about a character, then "talk" about him or her to your readers as though telling someone about your grandfather or grandmother.

Write audibly. Read your work aloud and ask yourself: "Does it flow? Does it have a comfortable tempo and rhythm?" If having trouble getting started, **write "bullet points,"** short, pithy statements to be strung together later into full paragraphs. Respect grammar but respect your reader more. Use contractions and common phrasing to create a conversational feel in your narrative.

Insert humor. Remember the old adage *truth is stranger than fiction*? It is often more humorous as well. Don't be afraid to recount funny incidents, as long as they don't belittle or embarrass those involved. Save punch lines or humorous surprises for the last line, or even better, the last syllable.

Make it easy. Allow readers to enjoy the narrative without stopping to think about facts or figures. Convert statistics for easy reading (*four out of five* rather than *eighty percent*), change dates to years (*40 years ago* rather than 1978).

Obviously, specific dates and statistics are crucial for any local church history. Picirilli advises the use of tables for moderators, pastors and deacons, important dates, and more to keep the narrative from becoming cluttered with numbers while still retaining important statistics for historical record. Information graphics present dry, statistical data in ways both engaging and visually pleasing for readers. Historian Hugh C. Bailey believes statistical tables are a valuable element in local church histories because they "present at a glance the 'panoramic view' of changes in the church."[31]

Answer the questions. Few things are more frustrating to readers than missing details. Don't leave them hanging. Provide facts by answering age-old journalistic questions: *who, when, what, how, where,* and *why.* When questions are answered, don't stop writing; *conclude* writing. Wrap things up in a way that fulfills the reader's curiosity, even when that doesn't translate to a happy ending. Finally, do your best to create an easy transition for the next writer of your church's history.

Cut the clichés. Sportscasters are infamous for corny one-liners: "It's crunch time!" "It's a nail biter!" "The crowd goes wild!" "He could—go—all—the—way!" While clichés work well for these colorful characters, they are cumbersome, even boring, in print. If you use a cliché, make it deliberate and humorous.

Avoid "church-speak." These words and phrases leave non-churched readers scratching their heads in bewilderment. They cannot help but wonder about statements such as *walked the aisle, got saved*, or *on fire for God* (sounds painful). Consider some alternatives. For *born again,* substitute *followed Jesus;* replace *winning souls* or *evangelizing* with *expressing your faith* or *telling others what you believe*. Do your best to restrict church-speak and colloquialisms to quotes acquired in interviews. You will soon discover those quotes provide a treasure trove of colorful phrases for your project.

Make it unique. In Ecclesiastes 1:9, the writer pondered, "There is no new thing under the sun." No matter what you say, it likely has been said before and will be said again. So, make it memorable. Find a new angle. Write from a unique perspective. The greatest writers are those who learn to write from beyond their own experience, to express things from a fresh viewpoint.

Be your toughest critic. Review each page or chapter carefully. Ask an honest friend (preferably one proficient in English grammar) to review your work and then humbly accept the advice. Watch for and correct awkward phrasing, passive verbs, ambiguous or overused words, and discrepancies in chronology or characters.

Rewrite rigorously. Don't be naive about writing; it is hard work. It takes practice. It requires discipline. It demands skills developed only by writing. Master basic grammar and keep a style guide on your desk. Wear out your online dictionary. Get to know the thesaurus. On the bright side, by the time you finish this project, you will qualify as a veteran writer.

FOUR GRAMMAR NOTES

While this book does not pretend to be a grammar textbook or editorial style guide, four guidelines will help you avoid frequent grammar gaffs:

Destroy commas and kill exclamation points. Inexperienced writers overuse these common punctuation marks. Use them sparingly. Reserve exclamation points for *truly* exclamatory statements or points of emphasis. Follow this simple guideline: no more than two exclamation points per chapter (and never more than one at the conclusion of a sentence).

Limit adverbs and adjectives. Many are unnecessary. For example: "He clenched his teeth tightly." Can you "clench" any other way?

Learn and exercise the proper use of the following word pairs considered the most problematic in the English language:

- *Your versus you're. Your* indicates possession while *you're* reduces you are to contraction form.
- *Its versus it's. Its* indicates possession while *it's* is a contraction of *it is.*
- *Their, there, and they're. Their* "belongs" to someone; *there* is "where"; and *they're* abbreviates *they are.*

Finally, stop when you're done. Dodge overdramatic endings: hymns, poems, verses, churlish quotes. Avoid cliffhangers, unless you are planning to publish the sequel within three years. Few things are more frustrating than a story with no ending or a proposition without a conclusion.

Robert Morgan offers practical advice for new writers: "Subscribe to *Writer's Digest* and learn more about the craft of writing. Take a night course at the local community college. Attend a writer's conference. ***Writing is a skill that must be learned and honed.*** If you are going to plant a garden, you must learn what grows in your area and how to care for it—basic horticulture. The same is true for writing."

Quick Tips for Better Writing

- Write to communicate, not to impress.
- Start fast. Grab the reader's attention.
- Find your focus; get to the point.
- Write lean: short words, sentences, and paragraphs.

- Use descriptive, exciting verbs.
- Write like you speak.
- Read your work aloud.
- Write a picture.
- Use contractions and common phrasing for conversational effect.
- Tell stories, not facts.
- Answer the questions: *who, when, what, how, why,* and *where.*
- Cut clichés and church-speak.
- Write for your reader.
- Find a unique perspective.
- Take a second (and third) look.
- Rewrite rigorously.
- Stop when you are (or should be) done.

Common Formatting Mistakes

Avoid these common mistakes when formatting body text:

- Hyphens for bullet points
- Hyphens for dashes
- Underlining (anything, even titles or Web addresses)
- *Italics* for emphasis rather than ALL-CAPS
- Two spaces after a period
- Periods outside the quote mark (never, unless you move to England)

PROOFING AND REVISION

Perhaps the hardest work of writing comes after the first draft has been completed, yet Robert Morgan believes rewriting is the most important part of writing. Effective revisions often make the difference between a good project and a *great* one. Most authors have their own proofing and revision process. Professional writers often rely on a team of editors, while amateurs rely upon their own sharp eyes and the help of grammar-minded friends. Some writers prefer to proof and revise as they go. Others wait until the entire manuscript is in place to begin proofing and revision.

Robert Morgan shares an "inside look" at his own revision process: "I don't do much proofing and rewriting once the book is done because I tend to edit along the way. I like to get every chapter and section of the book just the way I want before I move on to the next. If I wait until I have the entire manuscript in front of me, I find it too exhausting to go back and start from page one. Incrementally, it is manageable."

While the technique and timing of proofing and revision may vary by writer, most proofing includes four stages: *first read, text edit* (revisions and corrections), *second read* (proofing from someone other than the writer), and *final proof.* Each stage holds its own unique purpose in refining a rough manuscript.

First read. Most successful writers recommend working quickly. "Just get it down on paper," urges Phillip Morgan. Picirilli agrees, observing, "I simply start writing...just get it down." Pinson, too, admits to "working in bursts of creative energy." This quick-writing advice is valuable. Momentum is a writer's friend. Working rapidly keeps the author from becoming mired in details or, better yet, from looking ahead to see what remains to be written.

While quick work is commendable, in many cases, it also results in a messy and sometimes muddled first manuscript requiring the first read. After completing the manuscript, the writer should lay the project aside, take a day off—two, if the deadline allows—and enjoy time to exhale. With mind and body refreshed, return to the manuscript. Read it from start to finish, without interruption if possible. During this first look, remain alert for five problem areas: 1) contradictions; 2) problems with the flow of the narrative; 3) repeated or misquoted quotations; 4) glaring omissions; and 5) significant structural issues such as out-of-sequence paragraphs or chapters with weak endings. Circle each major problem and make notes about why it has been marked.

During the first read, strive to remain focused on content and avoid being distracted by grammatical errors or typographical mistakes. Many writers simply cannot (and probably should not) overlook these things. This is understandable. The key is not to stop and correct the errors immediately. Make a small mark beside each grammatical or typographical mistake and keep moving forward. Allow one exception to this rule: during the first read, and in *every* stage of proofing, circle each passive verb encountered. When an active replacement comes to mind, immediately jot it in the margin to be inserted later.

Paper or screen? Is proofing, correction, and rewriting more efficient when done onscreen or by hand on paper? While some might wonder if these methods split down generational lines, the reality has more to do with individual preference. Many younger writers, editors, and proofers prefer paper, while other, more experienced writers, prefer to edit onscreen.

The key? Make proofers happy. Allow them to edit onscreen by providing a digital copy of the manuscript file. (Be sure to copy your file for your proofer and keep the original.) Or, deliver a crisp, clean paper copy if preferred. Certainly, onscreen editing is more time efficient, but the method of proofing is not a moral debate. In the long run, it is far more important to keep your proofers (especially volunteers) happy in their work.

Text edit. After completing the first read, take a break then return to the manuscript. Start by correcting the major problem areas circled during the first read. Clarify apparent contradictions, restructure the narrative, correct inaccurate quotations, find and insert missing information, and straighten out structural inconsistencies.

Just because a paragraph or section of a chapter does not fit the flow of the manuscript, do not discard it. It may fit well in another section of the book. Robert Morgan follows a practical process for retaining and organizing these valuable misfits. He keeps a file he calls "the cutting room floor." Everything he removes from a project goes into the file. "In time," he notes, "I may choose to bring these sections back into the main story. I *never* discard them, because I may find the place they fit."

Read It Aloud

One of the most helpful proofing tips is to read the manuscript aloud. Reading aloud often reveals problems with text flow and pacing or pinpoints troublesome words that might have been overlooked. The human ear often reveals problems the eye does not catch. Reading aloud also keeps the mind from wandering, making it more difficult—though not impossible—to fall asleep on the job.

Once glaring textual and narrative issues have been resolved, return to the beginning of the project and work through it systematically, once again addressing each grammatical or typographical error marked during the first read. Replace passive verbs with active verbs. Correct punctuation. Eliminate exclamation points and extra commas. Then brace yourself. With text edits complete, the time has come to hand over the book to several brutally honest friends for proofing.

Second read. Enlist the help of at least two proofreaders (and preferably more). Take a deep breath and ask them to read your work closely and critically. At this stage in the process, it is crucial to shelf your ego. Calmly consider their corrections. Carefully contemplate editorial suggestions. The team approach to proofing and revision, while painful for the writer, only makes the finished project stronger.

Robert Morgan acknowledges that every writer experiences moments of dismay when he or she encounters criticism. During the editorial phase of his bestseller, *Reclaiming the Lost Art of Meditation,* Morgan's editors were so nervous about his comparisons between the transcendental meditation of the East and the transformational meditation of Scripture, they removed significant portions of his work. "I have to admit I was a little frustrated," Morgan confesses, "but I also understood they knew their audience, so I trusted them."

It was the right call. In time, the book was recognized as one of the most influential evangelical books of the year. "Further proof it is usually best to trust your editors," Morgan concludes.

Final proof. After second corrections are completed, return to the manuscript for a final read before passing the project to designers. During this final excursion through the text, pay close attention to headlines, footnotes, names, titles, Scripture quotes, and references. However, don't waste time on awkward page breaks or page numbering, as pagination and page structure will change during the design process.

Congratulations! With planning, researching, writing, reading, rewriting, proofing, and finishing touches complete, you can breathe a sigh of relief as the "heavy lifting" shifts to the shoulders of the designer.

CHAPTER SIX

DESIGN BASICS

To set forth in order...(Luke 1:1).

While the creation of a local church history focuses primarily on planning, research, writing, and promotion, the importance of good design and effective use of photography cannot be overstated. Research is the cornerstone, the foundation of the project. Writing supplies the walls and ceiling. Good design "welcomes the reader home" into the story of your congregation. It paints the walls, arranges the furniture, and even hangs the pictures—little touches that set the stage for the tale being told.

While it is true few writers of local church history also serve as designers for the project, understanding basic design principles will help the writer communicate his or her wishes regarding layout. These principles help identify good and bad design and lead the writer or team to ask questions a designer will both understand and respect.

This chapter provides an overview of basic design principles, lists common design mistakes to avoid, explains elemental principles of layout, and offers guidelines for choosing and implementing photography and graphics effectively. First, consider some "straight talk" about working with designers.

WORKING WITH DESIGNERS

As a former publishing company art director, I am a fan of designers. They are brilliant, creative individuals with the ability to take a rough concept and transform it into a work of art. Over the years, however, I have also learned several key principles to remember when working with designers or other creative personalities.

Give yourself a cushion. Before seeking out a designer, establish a firm deadline by working backward from the release date and "subtracting" time needed for printing and binding (sixty to ninety days as a general rule, but check with the printer). Subtract two additional weeks from this schedule—just for good measure—to determine the design deadline. Designers are notorious for pushing deadlines. In pursuit of artistic excellence, chances are they will refine their work right up to the moment they hand it over. This attention to detail is what makes them good at what they do. It also sometimes makes them late.

Ask for a project bid. When working with designers, as with writers, request a bid on the entire project rather than an hourly rate. The incentive to work quickly is removed when the individual is paid by the hour. Avoid paying the entire design fee up front, although a partial payment is an accepted industry standard. If the project is extremely time-sensitive, offer incentives for an early finish date. Request benchmark reviews, the possibility to look over sections of the project in increments. This approach keeps the designer on track and prevents one portion of the book from receiving all the attention.

Discuss revisions. Make it clear whether the designer will be expected to make requested editorial and design corrections to the layout. Ensure that revisions have been included in the bid before agreeing to it. While most freelance designers assume two rounds of revisions when bidding (the industry standard), never assume this is the case—ask. Also, remember that revisions take time, and those days also must be subtracted from the design deadline.

Get it in writing. While an agreement with designers does not require a formal, notarized contract, it is helpful to *spell out in writing* the expectations of both the author (individual or church) and the designer.

After approving the agreement, both parties should sign and date the document. While this may sound severe, a written agreement helps avoid confusion or hard feelings from one or both sides and gives the church legal grounds to refuse payment if the designer fails to meet expectations (or vice-versa).

Don't be surprised or offended if the designer requests a contract. Contractual agreements are common practice.

Trust your designer. Reading this short chapter will not make you a designer any more than reading a car repair manual will make you a mechanic. When you hire a designer, trust him or her to do the job. Don't micro-manage. Avoid constant revisions based on the ever-changing whims of a committee. Store up "good will" for areas where obvious improvements are necessary and significant changes are requested. Select one or two church members who understand principles of visual communication and rely heavily on their advice. "Design by committee" is the quickest way to miss a deadline and infuriate a designer.

How will you recognize good design? Andrea Young, longtime graphic design manager at Randall House & D6 Family Ministry, observes that ***good design is design that fits the intended audience.*** If the design is received well by the committee, if the layout helps tell the story, and if the overall aesthetic appeals to readers, it is good design. "Good design doesn't always meet design standards," Young concludes. "The bottom line is whether it fits your story and your readers."

Say thank you. Designers often go unappreciated, especially when the individual has little connection to the congregation. Go beyond a simple credit line in the opening pages. Invite the designer to the special service where the book will be released. Be sure he or she receives a copy of the finished book. Remember, your designer may not be a Christ-follower. Let the story of your church, the story of changed lives, testify to God's grace and then reinforce that testimony through gracious interaction.

BASIC ELEMENTS OF DESIGN

Typography. Typography is the key to the designer's toolbox. Most conversations about typography begin with the font. The term *font* traces to the French term *fondre,* which described casting or molding of metal. Today, the word simply refers to the style(s) of text used on a page. Fonts are separated into four basic categories: *serif, sans serif, script,* and *glyphs.*

Serif fonts are traditional in appearance, with decorative marks or flourishes called serifs. These marks, carried over from the days of handwritten manuscripts, were thought to add beauty and readability to text. *Sans serif fonts,* literally *without serif,* contain strong clean lines, without the added marks or embellishments. *Script fonts* mimic handwriting, while *glyphs* (or "dingbats," as they are popularly described) replace letters with symbols or pictures.

Four Types of Fonts

Serif

Sans Serif

Script

✖❄❅❊▌ [dingbats]

During the design process, you may engage in a conversation about digital font file types. The following information will help you understand and contribute to the conversation.

Digital font typefaces come in three types of files: *postscript*, *true type*, and *open type* fonts.

For decades, *postscript fonts,* developed by Adobe, were considered the industry standard, allowing for high-resolution printing. Postscript fonts came with two files, the first for screen display, the second for printing. These font files did not cross platforms—that is, a different version of the font was required for use on Apple computers and another for PC computers. Today, postscript fonts are rapidly being phased out.

In time, single-file fonts containing both screen and print data replaced postscript technology. The earliest of these, *true type fonts,* were designed to cross platforms. Created by Apple and later licensed by Microsoft, both computing giants soon installed these fonts on new computers. While true type fonts lacked the print quality and resolution of their postscript counterparts, their convenience (and market share) quickly made them the most common file type.

Open type fonts bridged the gap between postscript and true type, offering single-file convenience with the high-resolution and capabilities of postscript fonts. Today, open type fonts have become industry standard. Although true type fonts remain widely used, open type is preferred by most printers. Postscript fonts have limited circulation and seem slated to join Beta-Max VCRs, eight tracks, and floppy disks as completely obsolescent. For more information about fonts and their history and development, visit www.adobe.com.

Readability. Consider the readability of text. Larger type does not necessarily equate to *readable* type. Readability begins at nine-point type, improves at ten, reaches maximum readability at eleven, begins to fall off at twelve, and gets much worse at fourteen points and larger. This assumes the reader has unimpaired vision and is reading print.

Leading and kerning. *Leading* refers to the vertical distance between lines of text and is generally measured in points, the same measurement used for type. In the days of metal type printing presses, printers inserted strips of lead (thus the name) between lines of type to separate them from one another. Leading is measured from the bottom of one line to the bottom of the next. The appropriate amount of leading is important for readability. Too much leading causes confusion about where to look; too little leading creates a dark and uninviting paragraph that can tempt the reader to skip the entire section.

Kerning (or *tracking* when applied to an entire line or paragraph) refers to the space between letters. Kerning affects readability as much as leading. Text with tight kerning becomes dense and unreadable; text with overly loose kerning makes it difficult to distinguish one word from the next.

Color. Good color contrast is crucial to readability. It is always preferable to place dark text on a white or light background. For most text-heavy local church histories, black type on white or cream paper is advised.

Most Readable Color Combinations

Black on White

Yellow on Black

White on Blue

Yellow on Blue

Green on White

Blue on Yellow

Young warns against the *worst* color combination for readers: red text on a blue background: "The human eye focuses on blue in the front retina and red behind the retina. That means reading red on blue can give readers a physiological headache."

For further resources on the latest trends and combinations of colors, visit color.Adobe.com. This web application generates color themes for any project. Experiment with color variations and browse thousands of color schemes submitted by designers around the globe.

Justification. While the term sounds theological, *justification* in design simply refers to the four basic alignments for blocks of text: *left, right, centered,* and *justified. Left justification,* aligning text to the left of the column, is more comfortable to read and less formal than full justification. *Full justification* (often referred to as *justified type*) stretches or compresses lines of type into a rigid column. While full justification creates smooth edges on the block of text, it often leaves awkward spacing that creates "holes" within the text and inhibits easy reading. *Right justification* is often used for pull-quotes, captions, or tables to break the monotony of left-justified text. *Centered text* can be effective for headlines, opening paragraphs, or captions anchored to the width of a photograph or graphic.

THE TEMPLATE

Establishing a page template provides a comprehensive design structure to be used by anyone working on the layout of the project. The template defines the most basic yet important parameters of the page: margins, dimensions, column widths, image placement, headline placement, body fonts, caption placement, and so forth.

Young notes that a good template allows the designer to organize, align, and arrange elements on the page in ways that give power and meaning, while increasing readability and visual interest. She notes this design is rooted in the text itself: "I read the content and then try to make the design reflect the story, theme, or feel of the content." Young offers three areas to consider when creating or reviewing the page template.

Margins. Young notes the margins establish the "feel" of the layout. She urges designers to consider carefully any items that must be included in the header and footer (top and bottom) of the page before settling on margin widths, warning, "If you have to go back and adjust page margins late in the project, it will change the entire structure of your book design."

She additionally warns against using same-width margins on all sides of the publication. For books or other facing-page documents, the inside margin should be smaller than the outside. The bottom margin is typically larger than any other. In books, the outside margins of the spread should double the inside. For the best appearance, margins should be sized progressively, from smallest to largest: inside, top, outside, bottom.

White space. Inexperienced designers often feel compelled to fill every "nook and cranny" of the printed page, using narrow margins and tight leading. However, negative space or "white space" is crucial for appealing page design. "White space is your friend," Young shares with a laugh. "As long as your budget allows, leave plenty of white space to make people want to read what you have written."

Always push white space to the outside of the page, away from the center. Leave generous white space around typographic and graphic elements. These simple steps ease visual tension for readers (not to mention eye strain) and invites them to continue reading. While it is true white space increases the page count, the extra pages may be the best investment in the design of the project.

Borders. Use borders to draw attention to important information (statistical tables, lists, pull quotes, etc). The use of borders is a great tool but should be limited for maximum effectiveness. Young suggests using the sharp edges of text columns or artwork to create the illusion of borders to avoid overuse.

When it comes to the template, Young concludes *simplicity* is the key. She advises designers to remember white space is a plus and to make the page design comfortable, reading naturally from top left to bottom right. "Don't insert too many photos. Don't let it get too busy. Don't let the design overpower the story. Just keep it simple."

SMART TEXT

The effective visual use of text on the page draws readers into a story and keeps them reading. This is especially important in a visual culture accustomed to video snippets, tweets, posts, eye-popping text, and flashing images. With today's non-readers in mind, consider suggestions for "smart text" that grabs and keeps the attention:

Use clever, eye-catching headlines, five to eight words in length. Be careful, however, not to use headlines that create visual interest but do not accurately communicate the story. Avoid "click-bait" (deliberately provocative headlines used to capture online readers through sensational claims).

Insert subheads or section heads to break up long portions of text into smaller, more manageable sections.

Use block quotes to separate quotations of five or more lines from the main text.

When using images, always include captions to clarify and support the image.

Use pull quotes (repeated or summarized statements from the text) to provide a visual break to a lengthy sections or to summarize page contents for readers.

Insert sidebars, tables, or information graphics to add interest to the page and support the content.

Use an alternate contrasting font to set captions, sidebars, and tables in a manner that distinguishes them from body type.

Avoid six common formatting mistakes that often make it into print:

1. Avoid *italics* in long blocks of text. Not only does the overuse of italics make text increasingly difficult to read, italics should be reserved for intended uses: points of emphasis, titles, terms being defined, and words in another language.

2. AVOID ALL CAPS unless you want to SHOUT at readers.

3. Avoid double spacing after periods. If you look closely at today's books and magazines, you will find only a single space between the period at the end of a sentence and the start of the next. A famous "typing class" rule of previous generations required two spaces after every period to offset the rigid letter spacing on typewriters, which made it hard for readers to distinguish between sentences.

With technological advancements, today's letters and words rest comfortably on the page. Most word processing and page layout programs automatically insert appropriate tracking and kerning. As a result, only one space is needed to mark the end of a sentence. The extra space feels awkward and disrupts reading.

4. **Avoid underlining,** even to designate Web links. Today, underlining—another relic of the typewriter era—has been replaced entirely by italics.

5. **Avoid using more than two font families per page,** and perhaps per book or project. Few design errors are more distracting than excessive typefaces. "The number one problem I see in design is using too many fonts," reflects Young. "Inexperienced designers go online and run across a million free fonts. Just because those fonts are there, and free, doesn't mean they have to use them. In fact, they shouldn't."

Many design experts recommend no more than two font families (Helvetica, Times, Palatino) per project, although they encourage using the various "faces" within those families: italics, bold, condensed, small caps, and so forth. Others, like Young, allow designers slightly more freedom. "Find your 'favorite five,'" she advises, "and limit yourself to those particular fonts in your work." A careful selection of complimenting typefaces will help readers sort out information visually and navigate the book. Too many typefaces result in visual confusion. Still need convincing? This book uses only two fonts: *Open Sans* and *Merriweather*. They are simply used creatively.

6. **Avoid using similar fonts together.** When selecting primary fonts, use font faces that compliment and contrast by their variety (Times and Helvetica) rather than confuse due to similarity (Times and Garamond). Consider using a serif font for the main text (for ease of reading) and a sans-serif font for headlines, sidebars, and pull-quotes. If the body font is heavy or

dark on the page, experiment with a lighter font for headlines. The general appearance of fonts on the page sets the mood for your book almost as much as readability.

PHOTOGRAPHY AND GRAPHICS

The familiar idiom *a picture is worth a thousand words* may be an exaggeration but only slightly. With local church history, the value of a well-placed, well-identified photograph is immeasurable. Good photography brings life to the story and gives readers faces and places to go with names and dates.

"Pictures 'ground' history," notes documentarian Victor Albright. "They connect history to daily life." When used appropriately, a good photograph can set the mood and context for the accompanying narrative. Explore three areas regarding this important topic: *understanding digital files, choosing good photographs,* and *pursuing visual storytelling.*

UNDERSTANDING DIGITAL FILES

Pixels versus vector. Designers use two types of images in their work. *Pixel* images consist of tiny dots called—you guessed it—pixels. The number of dots contained in each square inch is referred to as the dpi, or dots per inch. The number of pixels contained in an image reflects the quality of the file. Images with high pixel counts are described as high resolution. As the dimensions of a picture increase, the existing pixel data is spread out to fit those dimensions, and the quality of the picture is reduced. When a picture with a low pixel count is used for publication, the image may appear grainy or blurry.

Historic photographs must be converted into digital format

by scanning. During scanning, it is crucial to adjust settings to no less than 300 dpi. If a picture has been selected for a cover or feature page, consider scanning at 450 to 1,200 dpi, depending on the capabilities of the scanner. Don't be surprised or offended if designers request the original photographs rather than accepting your scans. Many design firms and freelance designers use high-end equipment to maximize the potential of photographs.

Unlike pixel images, *vector* images are created using solid blocks of color based on geometric ratios. These images can be scaled to enormous dimensions without losing resolution or quality, making them ideal for large projects. Why mention these "billboard" images in a discussion of local church history? Most logos and information graphics are created using vector-based software.

CMYK versus RGB. You will likely encounter these common color designations during the design stage of your project. CMYK refers to the four colors used by a traditional four-color printing press: cyan, magenta, yellow, and black. RGB stands for red, green, and blue—the colors used on screens, from phones and tablets to televisions and computer monitors.

For many years, printers required artwork and photography to be converted from RGB to CMYK format in preparation for printing. More recently, with the introduction of the digital press, most printers accept both RGB and CMYK files. Don't assume this is the case. Ask the printer which color format is preferred and relay this information to the designer.

Output. Designers must prepare output files to deliver to the printer. Most printers have their own file preparation requirements, ranging from high-end PDF files to native files (Adobe InDesign, Quark Xpress, and others) and requiring any linked images and fonts.

While it is not important for you to have a technical understanding of output file specifications, as the project manager, it is important to ask your printer what is preferred.

Relay file information to the designer on the front-end of the design process or provide contact information for the printer. These requirements may affect the program used by the designer or the way files are processed and handled. Unexpected surprises can cause unnecessary delay.

CHOOSING GOOD PHOTOGRAPHS

Judges at a photography contest consider a "laundry list" of criteria to help identify the best shots: focus, depth of field, contrast, density, lighting and effects, balance, harmony, attention to the rule of thirds, diffusion, exposure, and much more. When selecting pictures to accent a local church history, however, it is unlikely you will work with award-winning photography. Instead, the photographs at your disposal may be limited to scratched and dirty nineteenth-century stereographs, 1970s Polaroids, and a scattering of smart phone selfies.

Phillip Morgan encourages historians not to be discouraged by their selection of pictures, noting, "When you write about history, you live under the tyranny of the archive. You are limited to what you have, and you can use only what you have." He adds with a chuckle, "If you have horrible pictures, you must use those horrible pictures or leave them out altogether." Understanding this reality, simplify the standards for selecting good pictures. Search for pictures that meet four criteria: *focus, contrast, implied motion,* and *visual storytelling.*

Focus. When it comes to historical photographs, focus doesn't necessarily refer to clear-cut, well-defined pictures with no blurring and sharp edges (all great characteristics). Instead, *focus* refers to a picture with an immediate point of connection—a person, group, building, or action that draws the eye immediately. Focus is especially powerful in pictures where a single individual seems to make eye contact with viewers, pulling them into the picture and the world it represents.

Contrast. Many historical photographs, and even some modern photographs, are overexposed or deeply faded. Unless this type of photograph is vital to the story, find another picture with greater contrast (variation between light and dark). Good contrast helps draw the viewer's eye to the desired focus of the picture. Professional photo correction is always an option, but prepare to pay premium prices for this high-end skill.

Implied motion. Victor Albright notes most early photographs were staged because of the amount of time required for exposure. (As evidenced by the lack of smiles in the pictures; subjects simply couldn't smile long enough for the picture to be exposed.) Albright encourages historians to look for rare early pictures that don't feel staged but convey an evocative moment frozen in time. (This advice applies to modern photography as well.) The best pictures imply action or emotion.

Consider some iconic photographs: the victorious sailor kissing his girl in Times Square on V-J Day at the end of World War II; the courageous Chinese protestor facing down tanks in Tiananmen Square; the first steps of the moon landing;

15-year-old Hazel Bryan screaming at Elizabeth Eckford during the first day of school desegregation in Arkansas during the Civil Rights Era.

Each of these familiar images captures motion frozen in time. They transport viewers to the moment, put them in the crowd, and inspire the emotions likely felt by the characters in the photograph. Albright observes, "The portraits often used in history books are important, but images that evoke a particular emotion and raise more questions about the story are better."

Visual storytelling. "Any picture that tells a story is important," Albright advises. "You can write a historical fact, and alone it is soon forgotten. But when you connect that fact to a great picture, you bring it to life. You give it context and make it memorable. You make it part of the story."

This quest for pictures that tell a story is reflected by Albright's process for selecting good photographs. He goes through pictures until he encounters something striking, something that makes him ask, "What were they doing?" or "What were they thinking?"

Phillip Morgan, co-author of *Light and Truth: A Seventy-Fifth Anniversary Pictorial History of Welch College*, follows a similar process, selecting attention-grabbing photos that speak to the reality of things in that particular moment. "These images capture the tension of real life," Morgan observes, "but more importantly, they capture a unique aspect of the story I am telling."

Morgan urges the writer or historical team to wait until the rough draft has been completed before choosing pictures to complement the project. "This way, you can identify 'key players' or 'key moments' from the storyline." As you look for these story-telling images, identify pictures that represent a wide range of church experience (Sunday School classes, booster band, youth group, dinner on the grounds, river baptism) anything that pulls the reader into the story of the church.

Should some photographs be avoided? Yes. Avoid pictures that paints subjects in a bad light: awkward facial expressions, immodest positioning, or implication of questionable behavior. Morgan suggests additional types of photographs to avoid: pictures too scratched or creased for easy viewing, photographs that don't make sense or offer anything to the story, and photographs in which no one can be identified. "Captions are crucial," he concludes. "Try to use pictures featuring individuals who can be identified. Perhaps not everyone, but enough to connect the picture to your story."

One final note regarding photo selection: **avoid copyright infringement.** It is never acceptable to download or copy images for your project from the Internet (even when the photograph features your church or congregation) unless the website states clearly the image is in the public domain, or the site provides a fair use disclaimer. For more information on safeguarding against improper use of intellectual property, refer to *Appendix B.*

CHAPTER SEVEN

PROMOTION AND DISTRIBUTION

Even as they delivered them unto us...(Luke 1:2).

After seemingly endless months of hard work, the long-awaited moment finally arrives. You tear open the crisp cardboard box with trembling hands and carefully remove the first copy of your local church history. After pouring a fresh cup of coffee, you escort the new treasure to your favorite recliner, where you flip through page after page, marveling at the culmination of your efforts.

After satisfying yourself that all pages are in sequence, no pictures are missing, and every team member and volunteer was included in the credits, you lean back in your chair and sigh deeply. With a satisfied smile, you think, in true superhero fashion, "My work here is done!"

Then your gaze shifts to the fifty boxes of books stacked

precariously against your living room wall, and you are jolted back to reality. Momentary euphoria dissolves into sudden despair as the question slowly dawns upon you: "How will we *ever* get rid of these?"

Promotion is the final step in "building" your church history. Research laid the foundation. Writing supplied the walls and ceiling. Good design added the paint and furnishings. Promotion gives your project "curb appeal," making it attractive to potential readers. This chapter explores five promotional strategies to keep those boxes from becoming permanent décor in your home: start early; engage the congregation; create incentive and urgency; advertise creatively; and make the release of the book an event to remember.

After defining how a good promotional strategy leads to healthy book sales and reduces the stacks in your home, the final pages of the chapter offer a short list of alternative platforms for distributing your local church history to the broadest number of readers: e-books, PDF files, third-party publishing platforms, and the Internet.

STRATEGIES FOR PROMOTION

Start early. Chapter one stressed the importance of planning ahead. You will enjoy the results of that planning during promotion. Good promotion begins long before the first hour spent in research and writing. Ron Hunter notes good promotion spends 75% of time in planning and 25% in execution. "Every project needs a plan," he advises, "whether a script for a video or the table of contents for a book. If you spend appropriate time planning, most promotion will already be done when the final product is delivered."

> **If you spend appropriate time planning, most promotion will already be done when the final product is delivered.**
> **—Ron Hunter Jr.**

Consider two shortcuts to good promotion during the planning phase. *First, pick the right day.* Publish your local church history in conjunction with an anniversary, milestone, or special day at church. As noted in chapter one, these events produce a natural excitement and curiosity about the life and legacy of the church. Once the special day has been identified, verbally connect the book to that special day every time it is mentioned. Build a connection between the book and the day.

Second, set the date in stone and never deviate from it. A "solid" date provides a clear point of anticipation for potential readers, and it doesn't hurt to build accountability for the team while the book is researched, written, and produced. Most authors or teams experience moments of discouragement during this long and sometimes difficult process. At times, a well-publicized release date may be the only thing that keeps the project moving forward.

Engage the congregation. Inform church members about the project and keep them updated on progress. Share your own contagious excitement regarding new discoveries (although be sure to hold some back for the book). Ask members to serve on a historical committee or to assist with the project. Interview them about their memories at the church. Enlist Sunday School classes (especially seniors) in the search for historical records, books, materials, and photos. Use the congregation as a resource for identifying unknown individuals in historical photos. Find individuals with special talents in grammar, writing, art, and photography and enlist them as members of the historical team.

Possibilities are endless for engaging the congregation in the project; take full advantage of them. Excitement rises with each new person you involve in the creation of your history, and this connection with the congregation is the key to good promotion. Hunter observes the congregation will read your story when "they identify with the pain and struggle...and when they relate to what you are writing."

He warns against underestimating the power of personal connections when it comes to promotion and notes that, when the congregation becomes personally involved with the book, selling it will be no trouble. "People don't have much time these days," Hunter concludes. "So, connect the book to them and let them know *why* should they give ten precious hours to reading your work."

Create incentive and urgency. Consumers buy when they have incentive to buy. You've seen the lines of people waiting—sometimes camping outside in frigid weather—to buy the latest smartphone. You've witnessed the frenzy to find and purchase the latest "it" toy before Christmas. You've watched the commercials advertising limited editions, one-time offers, and "get them before they are gone" products.

How does one create this type of incentive and urgency when promoting a local church history? Emphasize limited availability. Remind listeners regularly that books will be available only in limited quantities (urgency). Offer incentives for pre-orders by reducing the cover price slightly, including early purchasers in a list of supporters printed in the book, or by offering a small historical memento for each advance purchase (incentive). Sign and number the first fifty copies and print special book covers for these volumes. Designate them as limited editions (incentive *and* urgency). If the special editions increase the cost of production, simply pass that expense along to purchasers. Many people will happily pay more to be part of an "exclusive" group.

Hunter shares one last piece of advice about creating urgency: "You have to show people a problem they have that the book will solve. Henry Cloud [author and psychologist] once said 'People never change until the pain of staying the same becomes greater than the pain of change.' He's right....Identify why your congregation *needs* this book."

When it comes to local church history, what is that need? Members of the congregation need to know their heritage and understand their "roots." This book will provide answers to their questions and give them greater insight into their family of faith. If you question the value of this curiosity about the past, consider the overwhelming number of recent television ads for gene testing or genealogical research sites. The current generation's curiosity about its heritage has made these resources one of the fastest growing "products" today.

Consider one warning about creating incentive and urgency for promotional purposes: never sacrifice your integrity (and more important, your church's integrity) to sell the book. If you advertise a limited print run, don't go back to press if you sell out earlier than expected. If you offer fifty limited-edition copies, don't print fifty additional copies. And, if the limited edition copies don't sell, resist the urge to reduce the price. The same purchasers happy to pay extra for the limited edition will be furious when someone else walks away with a bargain on the same product.

Advertise creatively. Your promotional plan should include all traditional advertising methods—verbal and written announcements, flyers, bulletin inserts, posters, tweets, and posts. These "tried and true" methods are important because it often takes five to seven visual reminders to motivate a potential purchaser to action.

Don't stop at "standard" advertising, however. Often, the most effective promotional methods are subtle and creative, engaging potential buyers unexpectedly and in unconventional ways. Be creative, starting with your promotional text. "Avoid generic descriptions such as 'It's a good book,'" Hunter urges. "Instead, tell them *why* it is a good book!"

Meet with the historical committee and devise clever ways to introduce the book to the congregation. The following suggestions will get the conversation started:

- Ask key characters in the book to read their stories during a church service as a testimony to the Lord's faithfulness.
- Enlarge a historical photograph of the congregation to banner size, hang it across the back of the church, in the vestibule or another highly visible area, and challenge the congregation to identify every person in the photo.
- During the weeks leading up to the release of the book, unveil a series of humorous pictures to appear in the book.
- Sponsor a church history trivia contest for adult Sunday

School classes then share the correct answers with the entire congregation.

Advertising creatively can be great fun. If you do it right, the congregation will enjoy themselves and begin to anticipate the release of the book, a win-win for everyone.

Make the release of the book an event to remember. Your church history book should become the cornerstone of the celebration. Have books engraved (if hardback), numbered, and signed for presentation to special guests: former pastors, denominational representatives, visiting city and state officials, and living charter members. Invite members of the Free Will Baptist Historical Commission to write an endorsement, attend the event, and speak to the congregation. Invite all guests to register for a door prize copy of the (limited edition) book. These commemorative activities say loudly to those who fail to pre-order: "This book is a big deal, and you *need* to buy it!"

ALTERNATIVE DISTRIBUTION

The big day has come and gone, and the book was a hit. The congregation expressed appreciation at learning the story of the church. Boxes no longer line the living room wall. In fact, the books are nearly gone, but requests keep coming.

Thanks to technology, several alternatives are available for publishing and distributing the history project beyond the initial printed copies: e-books, PDF files, publishing platforms, print-on-demand, and the Internet.

E-books. E-books (or electronic books) are designed for use with multiple screen sizes. Created in e-pub (electronic publishing) format, these files create a responsive design, similar to a reflexive website. Text reflows to fit any screen, from smart phones and tablets to laptops and large computer monitors. As the size of the screen changes, the number of words per page adapts, adjusting the length of the book accordingly.

E-books can be uploaded to the Apple Store, the Amazon Kindle library, or a wide variety of online vendors, making them a valuable and efficient tool for distribution. However, these files also have limitations. Though great strides have been made in e-pub technology, e-books still work best with books and documents consisting primarily of text. Pictorial histories or graphics-heavy documents should be reserved for other formats. E-pub files are not difficult to create; when the designer prepares files for the printer, simply request the extra step of creating an e-pub (.epub) document for distribution.

PDF files. Created in 1991 by John Warnock, cofounder of Adobe technology, along with a world-class team of computer programmers, PDF or *Portable Document Files* make documents visible across every computing platform. PDF files create an exact replica of the pages in the book or document—a "snapshot" including graphics, fonts, and margins, everything that makes your document unique. PDF files are searchable, can be password protected, and often contain live links that open web pages with a touch or click.

Like an e-pub file, creating a PDF file is not difficult, requiring only the touch of a key and the appropriate settings for intended use. While creating a PDF should not be a problem for the designer, be clear about how you intend to distribute the PDF file. Depending on the quality settings, PDF files can be quite large and not ideal for email or web distribution.

Publishing platforms. Third-party web publishing platforms bridge the gap between e-books and PDF files. These platforms take a PDF file (or various other output formats) and convert them into shareable, full-screen readers. Usually, these streamlined interfaces appear and function much like the apps created for smart phones, tablets, and computers. They are dynamic, flex to various screens, and offer live links and interactive features to readers.

Most digital interfaces read like a traditional book. Readers start with the cover and swipe (touch screen) or click to "open" the book or turn to the next spread of pages. The digital format also offers powerful features: enlarge or reduce text instantly; insert notes, pictures, and captions for a unique reading experience; and bring footnotes to life with live links to online content or web-accessible resources.

Dozens of digital publishing platforms are available, from www.issuu.com (currently the largest worldwide platform) to www.readz.com. At the rate digital publishing technology is evolving, another platform or technology type, may lead the pack by the time this book is published.

What is the downside to third-party web publishing platforms? The expense. Though competition in the growing medium has driven prices down, expenses still range from twenty to hundreds of dollars per month. While some platforms offer "free" services, most innovative features remain locked without a paid subscription.

Print-on-demand. If requests keep coming after the last history book has been distributed, consider print-on-demand services. As the name indicates, these short-run printers use digital presses to create small quantities of books, and some will print a single copy of your title. Printing on demand eliminates the need for a second press run that leaves surplus books that might go unsold.

Print-on-demand remains significantly more expensive than traditional printing, leaving little room for profit. However, if the church is concerned only with recouping expenses, and not in making money on the additional copies, print-on-demand provides a great option. Infinity Publishing, Ingram, BookBaby, Xlibris, and Westbow Press are among the largest print-on-demand companies. Most provide instant online bids for printing a book. Do the homework necessary to learn which company best fits your book at the most affordable price.

Internet. E-books, PDFs, third-party platforms—with all the new technology, an author or church can quickly create a digital "stack" of publications to offer readers. The church website provides a digital "bookshelf" for distributing any (or all) digital formats of your local church history. However, the potential of the Internet stretches far beyond the "bookshelf."

Consider incorporating abridged portions of your history into the church website. Reduce chapters to short stories or character sketches and create webpages featuring those sections. Then create a simple table of contents to guide visitors to their subjects of interest quickly and efficiently. Your printed church history suddenly will become an online book.

As you transform your local church history into Internet content, remember five simple guidelines for the web:

Make it fast. If your pages do not load quickly, your visitors will lose patience and leave. Keep entries, blogs, and pages short to avoid reader fatigue.

Be friendly and honest. Welcome readers to become part of your church story. Communicate clearly that your congregation is not perfect but growing in Christ.

Make it functional. Create pages that are easy to navigate and easy to use. Help readers find information quickly.

Keep it focused. Limit your visitor's choices. Lead them naturally through the site. Place the most important information in the center of the page. Place pictures where you want readers to look. Guide them to the important points you want to make.

Stay fresh. Few things are more frustrating than out-of-date websites. Make it clear you intend to update and expand your local church history content. Otherwise, why would anyone return for a second look?

What about video? While this volume limits itself to preserving and producing local church history in print or digital print format, Victor Albright suggests a video documentary as a good alternative for some churches. If the church has little written documentation, a video can focus on the stories of congregants. "The interviews themselves become the documentary," notes Albright, "while the narration provides summary, introduction, and segues between interviews."

Video also can help compile an overwhelming amount of research and information effectively. "You can cover a great deal of information much more quickly," Albright concludes.

Five Web Problems to Avoid

1. **Slow.** Do whatever it takes to keep your site fast. Find a new host. Cut back on graphics. Make it fast.
2. **Inflexible.** Your site should be flexible (dynamic) to fit all screens: phones, tablets, and computers.
3. **Confusing.** Ultimately, users want information. Make it easy to find.
4. **Constant motion** overwhelms readers. Simplicity encourages them to stay and read.
5. **Lengthy text blocks** will frighten away most visitors. Write with the Web in mind: subheads, bullet lists, highlighted keywords, short paragraphs, and simple writing.

CONCLUSION

TESTIFY TO THE NEXT GENERATION

That thou mightest know the certainty of those things, wherein thou hast been instructed (Luke 1:4).

We began this adventure in the opening verses of Luke's Gospel. While the apostle never had to worry about fonts, files, digital formats, or alternative distribution methods, this book has followed (and expanded) Luke's example of planning, researching, interviewing, and preserving history with integrity.

What was Luke's desired result for his efforts? In his final words of greeting to Theophilus, Luke shared his purpose: "That thou mightest know the certainty of those things, wherein thou hast been instructed (Luke 1:4)."

Directed by the Holy Spirit, Luke recorded his books to build the faith—the certainty—of believers, starting with Theophilus. He provided a detailed, well-ordered narrative built upon

Your local church history, or your own story...solidifies a legacy that will continue until the Lord comes again.
—Robert Morgan

firsthand accounts. Obviously, Luke took the right approach. His Gospel continues to testify to Christians more than two millennia later that they also have confidence in the things they have been taught about Christ.

This goal of testifying about God's grace and faithfulness to the next generation should be the same for us. "When you record church history, your local church history, or even your own story, it solidifies a legacy that will continue until the Lord comes again," concludes Robert Morgan. "I believe our greatest ministry takes place after we are gone. So much of what we do in a lifetime is 'sowing' in the people we meet and influence, in our families. And like seeds planted in spring, we can be certain of a harvest. Often, that harvest grows exponentially after we are gone."

Morgan points to the infinitely encouraging scenario of Hebrews 12:1–2, where the writer described a "great cloud of witnesses," the great heroes of the faith, whose testimonies continue to testify to us over the eons of time.

I pray that your hard work in preserving your local congregation's story of grace will continue to inspire each new generation of believers until the Lord's return.

May God bless your efforts as you do your part to testify of God's faithfulness to you and to your church.

APPENDIX A: MEET THE EXPERTS

Victor Albright is a media specialist for the A.O. Smith Corporation. A Welch College graduate, Victor previously worked as a videographer for IM, Inc. and as a member of the production team at Magnetic Dreams, a widely-acclaimed animation studio with projects ranging from *Sesame Street* and Marvel's *Ironman* to multiple award-winning music videos and commercials for Dell, Crayola, Samsung, and Chick-Fil-A. In 2011, Victor directed and produced the documentary *Honoring Our Heritage,* which celebrated the seventy-fifth anniversary of the National Association of Free Will Baptists, tracing its history and development.

Keith Burden was born the son of a Free Will Baptist deacon, December 10, 1953. Converted at age 12, Keith answered the call to preach four years later. He completed studies at Randall University in Moore, Oklahoma, in August 1972 and later earned a graduate degree at Moody Bible Institute. Ordained to the gospel ministry in 1975, Keith was an associate minister or pastor for 27 years. He served as assistant clerk and clerk of the National Association of Free Will Baptists for 22 years before being elected to the position of executive secretary of the denomination in 2002, where he served until 2019. While executive secretary, he also served as editor-in-chief of the denomination's official publication, *ONE Magazine.* Keith and his wife Debbie currently live in Locust Grove, Oklahoma.

Ron Hunter Jr. is executive director/CEO of Randall House & D6 Family Ministry and cofounder and director of the D6 Conference. He speaks regularly at conferences and serves as consultant for ministry and business organizations. Ron has written over 50 articles for various magazines and authored or co-authored six books: *Toy Box Leadership; Youth Ministry in the 21st Century: Five Views; The DNA of D6; Recalibrate: A New Measure for Family Ministry*; *About You, About Me: Generational Legacy Journal*; and *How to Find the Right Pastor.* A Welch College graduate, Hunter earned the MPA from University of Colorado and a Ph.D. from Gary Cook School of Leadership at Dallas Baptist University. Hunter additionally served as an infantry officer in the U.S. Army and pastored for a number of years. Ron and his wife Pam have two adult children and two grandchildren.

Michael Lytle is CFO of Randall House & D6 Family Ministry. A 1998 graduate of Welch College in Nashville, Tennessee, he has a wide range of accounting and financial leadership experience. In addition to his administrative role, Michael is a frequent contributor to www.RamblingEverOn.com, a website dedicated to the intersection of culture and ministry. He and his wife Diane have three children, Caia, Elliot, and Darius, and live in Ashland City, Tennessee.

Phillip Morgan is the curator of the Free Will Baptist Historical Collection housed at Welch College in Nashville, Tennessee, where he additionally serves as History Program coordinator and professor. A former small businessman, Phillip holds degrees from Middle Tennessee State University (M.A., History) and Welch College (B.S., Music Performance, Biblical Studies). His interests include theology, philosophy, architecture, gardening, music history and theory, and southern agrarianism. Phillip, his wife Megan, and their children live on a small farm in Robertson County, Tennessee.

Robert J. Morgan served over 40 years as a pastor at The Donelson Fellowship in Nashville, Tennessee. A best-selling and Gold Medallion-winning writer, he has more than 35 books in print with more than four million copies in multiple languages. He writes for David Jeremiah and *Turning Points* magazine and has numerous articles published in other leading Christian periodicals. He is a regular contributor to *The Huffington Post* and has appeared on numerous national television and radio shows. Rob and his late wife Katrina have three daughters and fourteen grandchildren.

Robert E. Picirilli is an author, retired college professor, and chairman of the Free Will Baptist Historical Commission. He received a B.A. from Welch College in 1953 and completed graduate studies at Bob Jones University, earning an M.A. in theology in 1955 and a Ph.D. in New Testament text in 1963. He additionally was awarded an honorary Doctor of Divinity degree by Bob Jones University in 1967. Picirilli's teaching career began at Welch College in 1955. He taught New Testament Greek and Interpretation for 47 years in addition to serving as registrar and academic dean on the undergraduate level and academic dean for the graduate program at his alma mater. Picirilli's published works include *Book of Galatians; Romans; Paul the Apostle; Grace, Faith, Free Will; Contrasting Views of Salvation: Calvinism and Arminianism; Discipleship: The Expression of Saving Faith; Free Will Revisited: A Respectful Response to Luther, Calvin, and Edwards; Teacher, Leader, Shepherd: The New Testament Pastor;* and, most recently, *God in Eternity and Time: A New Case for Human Freedom*, which was named among the most influential theology books released in 2022. Picirilli not only serves as general editor for the *Randall House Bible Commentary* series but also has authored commentaries on 1 and 2 Peter, 1 and 2 Thessalonians, Ephesians, Philippians, 1 and 2 Corinthians, and Mark. Picirilli is a frequent contributor to denominational publications and professional theological journals.

J. Matthew Pinson is Welch College's fifth president, having served in that office since 2002. A native of Pensacola, Florida, he attended Welch College in the 1980s and later graduated from the University of West Florida with a B.A. in humanities and an M.A. in history. Pinson received an M.A. in Religion from Yale University, where he met his wife Melinda, a North Carolina native who was also a graduate student at Yale. The two married in the summer of 1994 and began a pastorate in South Georgia. While there, he engaged in doctoral studies in history at Florida State University. After assuming the presidency of Welch College, Pinson completed a doctorate in higher education leadership from Vanderbilt University. He is author or editor of numerous articles and books, including *Perspectives on Christian Worship* (Broadman), *Four Views on Eternal Security* (Zondervan), *A Free Will Baptist Handbook* (Randall House), *The Washing of the Saints' Feet* (Randall House), and *Arminian and Baptist* (Randall House). The Pinsons have two children, Anna and Matthew.

Carol Pipes is director of corporate communications for LifeWay, where she previously served as manager of editorial services and editor of *Facts & Trends* magazine. For many years, she served as director of content development at the North American Mission Board and as editor of *On Mission* magazine. Pipes has received numerous awards and recognition for her work in Christian journalism and served as president of the Evangelical Press Association. In 2017, in conjunction with LifeWay's move to a new corporate headquarters, Pipes headed a team that documented the 125-year history of the organization.

Jack Williams was born in 1942 on a sharecropper's cotton farm in West Carroll Parish, Louisiana. Converted in 1958, at age 16, he accepted the call to preach eight months later and began a 60-year ministry using a borrowed Bible. After graduating from high school, Jack attended Welch College, earning a B.A. in theology in 1966. He continued his education at Sacramento Baptist Theological Seminary, completing an M.A. in 1973 and a Ph.D. from Louisiana Baptist University in 1976. From 1959-1969, Jack pastored churches in Louisiana, Tennessee, and Arkansas, before accepting a role as academic dean at California Christian College, where he remained eight years. In 1977, Jack began his life's work as editor of *Contact* magazine and executive administrator for the Free Will Baptist Executive Office. Jack earned a reputation for excellence in publishing. His writing was known for wit, journalistic fairness, and encouragement. His work as writer and editor earned 13 awards from the Evangelical Press Association and helped launch a fleet of new writers. In 2005, after *Contact* magazine ceased publication, Jack became director of publications for Welch College, where he remained until retirement. The beloved communicator died April 29, 2016.

Mary Ruth Wisehart spent more than 30 years as an educator at Welch College, until being elected executive secretary-treasurer of Women Nationally Active for Christ in 1985, where she remained until retirement. A 1955 graduate of Welch College, Wisehart earned three additional degrees (B.A., M.A., and Ph.D.) at George Peabody College. A prolific author, she authored *Sparks Into Flame: A History of WNAC* (1985), *Beyond the Gate: The Autobiography of Mabel Bailey Willey* (1998), revised the *WNAC Manual* (1995), and edited *The 50-Year Record of the National Association of Free Will Baptists* (1988), in addition to numerous magazine articles, columns, and editorials. Wisehart served ten years on the Free Will Baptist Historical Commission and additionally chaired the commission, the only woman to serve in either capacity. Wisehart died March 29, 2021.

Andrea Young has been the graphic design manager at Randall House & D6 Family Ministry since 2004. She earned degrees in graphic design and advertising from Pensacola Christian College. With more than twenty years in the industry, Andrea guides her designers through the production of more than 200 books and products each year, in addition to producing a constant stream of advertising and event design. The team has won numerous awards for their work, including Awards of Excellence from the Evangelical Press Association and top honors from the Printing Industry Association of the South (PIAS). Andrea and her husband Scott have two adult daughters, two grandsons, and live near Springfield, Tennessee.

APPENDIX B: FREE WILL BAPTIST HISTORICAL COLLECTIONS

Bates College
Edmund S. Muskie Archives and Special Collections
Free Will Baptist Resources
70 Campus Avenue
Lewiston, Maine 04240
207-786-6354
muskie@bates.edu
www.bates.edu/archives/bates-college-history/freewill-baptist-resources/

Harvard University
Harvard Library
Cambridge, Massachusetts 02138
617-495-1000
With a 76-library network, Harvard University has vast holdings, including a large collection of Free Will Baptist resources. For a comprehensive online catalog, visit **http://hollis.harvard.edu**.

Hillsdale College
Mossey Library
The Freewill Baptist Collection
33 East College St.
Hillsdale, Michigan 49242
General Inquiries: 517-607-2701
Circulation Desk: 517-607-2404
For a list of holdings: **http://lib.hillsdale.edu/file/Freewill-Baptist-Collection-Bib.pdf**

University of Michigan
Bentley Historic Library
1150 Beal Avenue
Ann Arbor, Michigan 48109
734-764-3482

Note: Bentley Library holds a limited collection of Free Will Baptist materials, but they have a significant collection of papers from the family of Ransom Dunn, Free Will Baptist theologian and founder of Hillsdale College in Michigan.

Mount Olive College
Moye Library
Free Will Baptist Historical Collection
644 James B. Hunt Road
Mount Olive, North Carolina 28365
https://moc.libguides.com (Free Will Baptist Historical Collection)

Randall University
Free Will Baptist Collection
3701 S I-35 Service Road
Moore, Oklahoma 73160
405-912-9000
http://rulrc.ru.edu

Welch College Library
FWB Historical Collection
1045 Bison Trail
Gallatin, Tennessee 37066
615-675-5255
Curator Phillip Morgan: pmorgan@welch.edu
Free Will Baptist Historical Commission Chairman Robert E. Picirilli: repicirilli@comcast.net

Access the Welch online database to search holdings. Use the *Limit Search Results* feature and select Collections/Historical Collection to narrow the field of your research:

http://f94016.eos-intl.net/F94016/OPAC/Index.aspx

APPENDIX C: INTELLECTUAL PROPERTY

What is "intellectual property" and why does it matter? In recent years, we have all become familiar with the ongoing debate regarding intellectual property, especially in the area of media. From the original culprit Napster to illegal copies crisscrossing the web today, the debate continues to rage about ethical and unethical behavior.

According to the U.S. Patents and Trademark Office, *intellectual properties* include any "creative works or ideas embodied in a form that can be shared or can enable others to recreate, emulate, or manufacture them."[32] Intellectual property is protected four ways:

- ***Patents*** provide individual rights for inventions up to 20 years.
- ***Trademarks*** protect words, names, symbols, sounds, or colors that distinguish goods and services. Trademarks, unlike patents, can be renewed forever as long as they are actively being used in business. Examples include the roar of the MGM lion, the pink of the Owens-Corning insulation, the Apple logo from Apple Computers, and the shape of a Coca-Cola bottle.
- ***Copyrights*** protect works of authorship, such as writings, music, and works of art that have been tangibly expressed. The Library of Congress registers copyrights that last as long as the author/artist/creator lives plus 70 years. Examples include: *Gone With the Wind* (novel and movie), Beatles recordings, and video games.

- ***Trade secrets*** are little known information that give companies an advantage over their competitors. The formula for Coca-Cola is the most famous trade secret.[33]

Stealing intellectual property is as much a crime as breaking into a home, stealing a car, or robbing a bank.

Obviously, writers of local church history are most interested in copyrights. This raises an important question: what is not protected by copyright?

- Ideas
- Common facts (not previously compiled)
- Titles, names, short phrases, slogans (unless trademarked)
- Lists of ingredients or contents
- Blank forms to record rather than convey information
- U.S. government publications
- Public domain works
- Items used under the guidelines of The Fair Use Doctrine

Under The Fair Use Doctrine of the U.S. copyright statute, it is permissible to use limited portions of a work, including quotes, for purposes such as commentary, criticism, news reporting, and scholarly reports. No legal rules permit the use of a specific number of words, a certain number of musical notes, or a percentage of a work for commercial or non-commercial publishing. Whether a particular use qualifies as fair use depends on the circumstances and intent.

This statement puts to rest the notion of a "set number" of words that can be used or quoted with no penalty. Copyright infringement is judged on a case-by-case basis, and greater leeway is given to academic and not-for-profit publications.

Legal is not always synonymous with ethical, however. Just

because writers or historians can "get away with something" does not mean they should. When using someone's intellectual property or quoting someone's work, take the extra steps to ensure you have been ethical in your approach.

- Find the primary source. Identify the original source of the information and determine if the material is in public domain.
- Contact the author or publisher and request permission to use the quote.
- Always cite your sources.

How do I protect my own work? Currently, copyright protection is automatic. According to United States copyright law:

1. Copyright arises on creation; neither legend (for works created after March 1, 1989) nor registration is prerequisite to the existence of copyright.
2. Legend is best practice: © [name of copyright owner] [date of publication]
   Example: © Eric K. Thomsen, January 2023.
3. Register your copyright with the Library of Congress.

APPENDIX D: HISTORICAL VIGNETTES

The following vignettes demonstrate some of the techniques and historical approaches taught in this book. They also provide a broad overview of Free Will Baptist history to share with your congregation during the months leading up to the publication of your own local church history.

Consider sharing these excerpts, or portions of these excerpts, in bulletins and newsletters, as historical flyers, on web posts, or as background material in your own project. You may be certain your own local church history will mean more to your congregation if they understand the greater Free Will Baptist story.

***Note:** Permission is granted to reprint, reformat, or adapt the information of Appendix D for personal, local church, educational, and ministry use with appropriate attribution. However, this information is not intended for resale purposes.*

THE FIRST BAPTISTS

(CHRONOLOGICAL NARRATIVE)

Free Will Baptists are one of the oldest religious bodies in the United States. They did not split from any other group, and they don't go back to a single person, time, or place. In fact, to trace Free Will Baptist origins, you must return to Elizabethan England before the colonization of America.

In 1600, most Christians were members of the Church of England, the official state church. (It wasn't legal to be part of any other church.) But state control had begun to crack, and religious dissenters gathered to worship on their own terms, with their own doctrine. In doing so, they risked their lives.

One group of dissenters fled London in 1607. Led by clergyman John Smyth, they escaped to Holland where they encountered two important doctrinal influences. First was baptistic doctrine that insisted infant baptism was not valid for salvation, that one should be baptized by immersion after an intelligent acceptance of the gospel. Smyth baptized himself and his followers, renouncing all ties to the Church of England. The group formed an identity as a congregation of "Baptist" believers.

The second significant influence was Dutch Arminian theology. Jacobus Arminius, after whom the doctrine had been named, rejected the prevailing Calvinistic views of his day, which taught that all events are pre-determined by God, including salvation, without freedom of choice for man.

In contrast, Arminius taught that men have free will, that Christ died for all, and that every man is free to accept Christ and be saved or to reject Christ and be lost. Smyth's group embraced this doctrine as the proper interpretation of Scripture.

In 1611, after religious persecution began to decline in their homeland, Smyth's Baptists, led by Thomas Helwys, returned to England. The date marks the founding of the first Baptist church on English soil. The group soon became known as "general" Baptists because they taught the Arminian doctrine that Christ died for all men, a general or universal atonement.

By 1633, a second Baptist congregation had been established. This group preached Calvin's doctrine that Christ died only for the elect. They were called "particular" Baptists. Before long, Baptist congregations emerged throughout England, some general, others particular.

FREE WILL BAPTISTS IN THE SOUTH

(CHRONOLOGICAL NARRATIVE)

The Baptist congregations established in the American colonies represented both general Baptists and particular Baptists. Baptist historians generally agree the earliest Baptist churches in America were general Baptist in doctrine.

Particular Baptists, however, were well-organized and more dogmatic in their preaching. Before long, their influence prevailed, and many general Baptist congregations swayed to particular Baptist doctrine. A scattering, however, maintained the doctrine of general atonement. These churches included the earliest "free will" Baptist churches in America.

A group of churches emerged in eastern North Carolina in 1727 (fifty years before the colonies declared independence from England) under the leadership of Paul Palmer. Little is known about the influences that contributed to Palmer's doctrine, but history records his ministry along the Chowan River, preaching general Baptist doctrine and establishing Baptist churches.

By 1752, sixteen churches were part of this fellowship. The "Palmer Movement" continued to expand until 1750, when particular Baptist preachers, led by John Gano of the Philadelphia Baptist Convention, proselytized the group. Most converted to particular Baptist doctrine.

Only four of Palmer's congregations remained true to the doctrine of their founder, but they became the nucleus for modern Free Will Baptists in the southeastern United States.

FREEWILL BAPTISTS IN THE NORTH
(CHRONOLOGICAL NARRATIVE)

In New England, the majority of churches were congregational, and Calvinism was the prevalent doctrine. In 1780, a young preacher named Benjamin Randall, converted under the preaching of George Whitfield, began preaching free will doctrine. He immediately found himself in "hot water" with the religious establishment.

Randall and his followers, no longer in good standing with their congregational church, organized a Baptist congregation in New Durham, New Hampshire, on June 30, 1780. The movement flourished. By 1820, Randall's followers had established 220 churches across New England and called themselves "Freewill Baptists." However, Robert Picirilli observes, "Long before 1780, believers of Arminian persuasion were mocked as 'free willers.' Historians of the northern movement agree this was first a term of derision, accepted only gradually and with reluctance."[34]

While no one knows *exactly* when Randall's followers officially accepted the moniker "freewill," Arminian doctrine was commonly referred to as "free will" doctrine. It was only logical for Arminian Baptists, whether Palmer's in the South or Randall's in the North, be described as "free will" Baptists.

The Randall Movement, named after its founder, grew rapidly and soon outstripped other Free Will Baptists in organization and expansion. Churches spread throughout New England and westward across Pennsylvania, Ohio, Michigan, and Illinois. By 1900, fifteen hundred churches in more than twenty states enjoyed an energetic foreign missions outreach, several educational institutions, and a thriving publishing ministry. Vigorous Freewill Baptist antislavery efforts were instrumental in the abolition movement, including the founding of Storer College in Harper's Ferry, West Virginia, the first college for freed slaves.

REVIVALISM, REFORM, AND FIERY PREACHING

(HISTORICAL HIGHLIGHTS)

Born out of the Great Awakening, northern Freewill Baptists found a comfortable home on the rapidly expanding American frontier. Founder Benjamin Randall, expelled from his Congregational church for preaching against Calvinistic doctrine, rejecting infant baptism, and teaching general atonement, quickly found himself welcomed by hardy men and women who were more concerned about daily survival than doctrinal minutia.

It is likely the very nature of Randall's "new" doctrine appealed to the adventurous, independent mettle of his rugged followers. Norman Allen Baxter observes that frontier New England was "a growing area and one that was peculiarly receptive to his [Randall's] preaching."[35] As a result, the denomination flourished in the revivalism and social reforms that characterized the Second Great Awakening.

Freewill Baptists played an integral role in this revival movement that swept the American frontier from 1790 to 1850. The movement fielded well-known evangelists and held many revival meetings in their churches. It hardly seems coincidental that the dates of the great revival coincide with the exponential early growth of the young denomination.

These "upstart" Freewill Baptists embraced numerous causes associated with this revival era, from abolition and temperance to Sunday School and foreign missions with great gusto (as might be expected from men and women with the fortitude to endure frontier hardships). Though most early Freewill Baptist preachers and evangelists had less education than Calvinistic counterparts, the simplicity of their preaching appealed to the pioneers.

According to Baxter, these pioneer preachers shared three characteristics: zeal and energy exerted in preaching and ministry; a willingness to embrace itinerant preaching methods; and hard-working lifestyles that kept them from burdening those to whom they ministered.

"They were farmer-preachers," Baxter concludes. "They farmed when they couldn't preach and vice versa. It was for this reason that sparsely settled areas, which could not possibly support a settled pastor, often heard the traveling Freewill Baptist preacher as he made his rounds."[36]

Through the work of these denominational pioneers, Freewill Baptists continued their western migration, bringing a message of free grace, free salvation, free will, and free communion to the American frontier.

FRONTIER MISSIONARIES

(CHARACTER STUDIES)

In late July 1822, David Marks, a Freewill Baptist evangelist from the Randall movement in New England, found himself several months into a mission trip into the rapidly expanding western frontier. After spending five days preaching near Portsmouth, Ohio, Marks made plans to cross the Ohio River to preach in Kentucky.

When the time came, the ferry used to cross the river was absent. Unwilling to miss his preaching appointment, Marks left his traveling companions and walked alone up the banks of the river. He found an old canoe cast up by a flood, and using a discarded plank for a paddle, Marks fearlessly pushed out into the Ohio. Things "went south" quickly (both literally and figuratively). The swirling currents of the river caught the tiny craft, tossing it back and forth and tearing a large hole in the bottom. In moments, water filled the canoe.

Just when Marks thought he would sink and drown, the canoe lodged in a large snarl of floating driftwood. Twisting helplessly in the current, Marks was carried downriver, far from his intended destination. He finally washed ashore back on the Ohio side of the river, landing at a settlement for slaves and former slaves. Determined not to miss an opportunity, Marks began to preach. His autobiography records that moment:

> *A large number, chiefly people of color, assembled, and I felt that Heaven assisted me in preaching. Their tears flowed freely, and my soul rejoiced for the privilege of pointing Afric's injured sons to the Lamb of God, who is able and willing to sanctify their wrongs to their eternal good.*[37]

Marks' remarkable story is but one among the many exploits of early Freewill Baptist missionaries who ventured into the American wilderness. John Colby, a young evangelist who began preaching revivals at age 21, recalled cutting holes in the ice to baptize shivering converts.

After hearing fiery evangelist Ransom Dunn preach, Freewill Baptist theologian George Ball remarked, "The young minister's preaching is like a tornado!"[38] In 1838 alone, at age 20, Dunn led 365 meetings and traveled more than 3,000 miles. During the twelve years that followed, Dunn preached thousands of times across ten frontier states, leaving a multitude of new believers behind him.

Black evangelist Charles Bowles and lady preacher Clarissa Danforth held services together, preaching to shocked and sometimes hostile congregations. Despite the challenges, God blessed their efforts, and many were converted.

These brave men and women and many others risked their lives for the sake of the gospel. As a result, Freewill Baptists grew and flourished across the American frontier.

A MOVEMENT IN UPHEAVAL

(MILESTONES)

In 1910–1911, the Randall Movement, by then renamed the General Conference of Free Baptists, merged with the Northern Baptist Convention and gave up its identity as a Free Will Baptist organization. Naturally, some churches refused to cooperate with the merger, especially in southern Ohio, southern Illinois, West Virginia, Missouri, and other points west. These scattered congregations gradually began to look to Free Will Baptists in the South for fellowship.

Additional Free Will Baptist groups continued to spring up sporadically throughout the southeastern states, often with little visible connection to other Free Will Baptists. One story from western Alabama documents how the first Free Will Baptist preacher from that state rode horseback to Carolina to be ordained before returning to organize a church in the area.

While it is impossible to trace development completely, by 1910–1911, when the Randall Movement merged with Northern Baptists, Free Will Baptist churches existed in the Carolinas, Florida, Georgia, Tennessee, Alabama, Mississippi, Arkansas, Oklahoma, and Texas with little connection to the Randall movement or one another. These churches were largely unaffected by the merger in the North.

From time to time, efforts were made to organize these churches. Many regional associations sprang up, only to fail. One association that lasted, however, was the General Conference, organized in 1921 in Nashville, Tennessee, with representatives from Georgia, the Carolinas, Tennessee, and Mississippi.

Another longstanding group named the Cooperative General Association, was organized in 1916 at Pattonsburg, Missouri. The Cooperative Association drew representatives from Missouri, Kansas, Nebraska, Oklahoma, and Arkansas.

Until 1935, the two organizations existed separately, one representing western Free Will Baptists and the scattering of Randall churches that did not merge with Northern Baptists. The other represented churches across the Southeast.

In November 1935, east and west met at Cofer's Chapel in Nashville, Tennessee, joined hands, and formed the National Association of Free Will Baptists. They intended to remain distinct from one another, but the unity, camaraderie, and cooperation they experienced made the separation unnecessary.

THREE DAYS THAT CHANGED HISTORY

(MILESTONES)

Delegates to the organizational meeting of the National Association of Free Will Baptists met at Cofer's Chapel in Nashville, Tennessee, November 5-7, 1935. Though these denominational pioneers met only three days, they conducted an impressive slate of business, putting aside previous differences to lay an organizational foundation that would stand for decades.

The voting body included representatives from various regional Free Will Baptist organizations, including the Eastern General Conference, the Cooperative General Association of the West, six state conventions, and 14 local associations. Officers were carefully selected to represent both East and West. They included John L. Welch from the General Conference, Winford Davis from the Cooperative Association, I. J. Blackwelder from the General Conference, and B. P. F. Rogers from the Cooperative Association.

Delegates quickly approved a constitution and bylaws, naming the new organization the National Association of Free Will Baptists. They established eight boards with five elected members to serve five-year terms. The boards, most still in existence today, included the Executive Board, Foreign Missions, Home Missions, Sunday School, Free Will Baptist League, Education, Superannuation, and Women's Auxiliary. The National Association, it was decided, would meet every three years to hear reports on the activities of each board.

In addition, delegates adopted a *Treatise of Faith and Practices*, approving the document by unanimous vote without hearing it read aloud, following a motion to that affect by Lizzie McAd-ams. Damon Dodd captured this pivotal moment in his book, *The Free Will Baptist Story:*

> *The motion was met with an immediate second, and the vote was overwhelmingly unanimous. This meant that the National Association of Free Will Baptists was now an official reality, that, at last, Free Will Baptists were united in a common cause. The entire congregation was caught up in the spirit of the momentous occasion. Strong men embraced each other and wept tears of joy and victory. The shouts of rejoicing Christians were lifted in praise to God.*[39]

A new chapter in the Free Will Baptist story had begun.

DOCTRINAL DISTINCTIONS

(THEOLOGICAL HIGHLIGHTS)

"Freewill Baptists are always on the right side of every moral question, and on the evangelical side of every controverted doctrine" (Henry Ward Beecher).[40]

The statement of faith adopted by the delegates at the 1935 organizational meeting of the National Association is nearly identical to the New England *Treatise* of 1869. The document spelled out in no uncertain terms basic tenets of the Christian Faith: the Trinity, Christology, biblical authority, general atonement, justification and sanctification, believer's baptism, the symbolic nature of the Lord's Supper, and the second coming of Christ. Several important distinctions, however, set Free Will Baptists apart from similar groups.

Free will and falling away. Two of these distinctions are reflected in the name of the denomination itself. *Free Will* points to the teaching of Jacobus Arminius that humans have free will to accept or reject the salvation offered to us by God's grace. This teaching stands in stark contrast to the doctrine taught by John Calvin, that God arbitrarily chooses or "elects" individuals to respond favorably to the gospel.

Free Will Baptists believe this freedom to accept or reject the grace of God continues after salvation, making it possible for a believer to reject his or her faith and become apostate, never to be reconciled to God. This doctrine clearly contradicts the popular notion of "once saved, always saved" prevalent among many Baptist groups.

Baptist. In its most basic meaning, the word *Baptist* indicates a belief in baptism by immersion. Free Will Baptists regard baptism as a symbolic gesture by which a new believer publicly acknowledges and aligns his or her saving faith with the death, burial, and resurrection of Jesus, thus becoming eligible for church membership. Yet, being "Baptist" goes beyond the simple act of baptism to include congregational church government.

The washing of the saints' feet. Perhaps the most visible (and unusual) denominational distinction is the washing of the saints' feet, usually practiced in conjunction with the observance of the Lord's supper. The practice, likely drawn from the influence of Dutch Mennonites and Anabaptists, commemorates the humility with which Christ Himself washed His disciples feet. Free Will Baptists regard this ceremony as a third ordinance (symbolic practice) instituted by God as a visual reminder of the atoning work of Christ.

From the beginning, feet washing created debate among Free Will Baptists. In their first *Treatise* published in 1834, New England Freewill Baptists indicated that individuals and local congregations would determine for themselves whether or not to observe feetwashing. The issue later became a barrier between the Eastern and Western Associations and even delayed the formation of a National Association from 1919 to 1935.

Since the 1935 meeting, however, the doctrine has remained in the *Treatise* unchallenged with one exception. In 1968, the Oklahoma State Association proposed a change to the wording, suggesting the removal of the phrase, "reminds the believer of the necessity of daily cleansing from sin." Although the resolution was approved, the *Treatise* remained unchanged.

Today, the washing of the saints' feet has become the most iconic and visible distinction of the Free Will Baptist movement. While the ordinance continues to set the denomination apart from other groups, in recent years, the number of churches that practice the ordinance has declined.[41]

THE CRUCIAL ROLE OF WOMEN

(CHRONOLOGICAL NARRATIVE)

"I request that the women of this body be excused to go to another room and organize a national body."[42]

The crucial role women played among Free Will Baptists began long before Fannie Polston of Nashville, Tennessee, made this request during the 1935 business meeting of the Eastern General Conference of Free Will Baptists at Black Jack Church in Pitt County, North Carolina.

The organized work of Free Will Baptist women can be traced to the early 1840s, when Ann Winsor of Providence, Rhode Island, formed the Freewill Baptist Female Missionary Society after hearing missionary Eli Noyes tell about desperate needs in India. The Woman's Missionary Society, as it came to be called, helped underwrite missions efforts in India, provided funding for Storer College in Harper's Ferry, West Virginia (started by Freewill Baptists to educate former slaves), and published *The Missionary Helper*, a news magazine distributed from 1878–1919. While the group eventually lost its identity when most northern Freewill Baptist churches merged with Northern Baptists, these early efforts set the pace for women in the Modern Era.[43]

During the early twentieth century, women's organizations in the South and West, though influential, were largely confined to local churches. Over time, they began to organize into regional groups to support foreign missions efforts. Later, their focus expanded to education, stewardship, temperance, and founding or supporting orphanages.

Two women emerged as leaders of the growing movement in the 1920s: Alice Lupton of New Bern, North Carolina, and Fannie Polston of Nashville, Tennessee. As Free Will Baptists pushed toward a unified denomination, these women worked feverishly to establish a corresponding organization for women. Women "won the race," and the National Woman's Auxiliary Convention (later the Woman's National Auxiliary Convention, Women Nationally Active for Christ, or simply WNAC) formed in June 1935, six months before the National Association.

Women embraced their role in the new denomination.

Despite limited funding, WNAC grew quickly. From the very beginning, WNAC identified its primary purpose as missions. According to Mary Ruth Wisehart, "WNAC has a missionary heart, a missionary purpose, and a desire to fulfill the great commission in every way possible."[44]

Starting in 1955, WNAC adopted a project-oriented strategy, uniting women for a single campaign each year. WNAC helped build a Bible Institute in India; a home for missionaries in Ivory Coast, West Africa; a missions station in Mexico; a home for missionaries in Japan; and provided furniture and supplies for a medical facility in Ivory Coast. The Nashville office received so many medical supplies that they eventually sent a letter to say, "Stop the offerings!"

In 1962, WNAC established the Missionary Provision Closet, a warehouse of linens, cooking utensils, and other domestic items to be distributed to missionaries going to the field or returning home. The project captured the hearts of Free Will Baptist women, and, today, the closet continues to supply the needs of both home and international missionary families.

"Through the years, Free Will Baptist women have contributed time, talents, money, and materials to get the gospel to the world," concluded Wisehart. "It would be impossible even to attempt to set down all they have done. Only God's records will show all the fruit produced by women who gave much because they loved much."[45]

JOHN WELCH AND THE "FREE WILL BAPTIST UNIVERSITY"

(CHARACTER STUDIES)

From earliest days, Free Will Baptists demonstrated great concern for education. A number of historic schools started and closed or joined other denominational groups. Only three regional Free Will Baptists colleges remained in operation by the 1920s: Ayden Seminary and College in Ayden, North Carolina; Tecumseh College in Tecumseh, Oklahoma; and Zion Bible School in Blakely, Georgia. By the time the denomination united in 1935, only Zion Bible School remained.

The lack of a unified college had long been a source of frustration. In 1907, representatives from Georgia, North Carolina, and Tennessee made efforts to open the Free Will Baptist University in Nashville. Unfortunately, only one student enrolled, and the new school came to an abrupt end. The frustrating attempt was not futile, for that single student, John L. Welch, soon became a major catalyst and spokesman in the push for a Free Will Baptist school. Appointed chairman of an Education Committee by the Eastern General Conference in 1921, Welch worked tirelessly through the 1920s and 30s to promote a college within the Eastern General Conference. He also met with representatives from the West (the Cooperative Association) to discuss the need for a school.

When the denomination organized in 1935, the first order of business for the newly elected Education Committee was to recommend Nashville as the location for a "Bible School" to start as early as 1936. Delegates named Welch, the moderator of the new denomination, to serve as the national secretary of education, heading a five-member Board of Trustees for a school that did not yet exist.

Plans were delayed, however. Four years later, during the 1939 National Convention in Bryan, Texas, Welch's daughter Jean, a 16-year-old high school student, delivered an impassioned plea to delegates. According to the minutes, "The challenge and prayer so gripped the hearts of all present that it resulted in a great educational rally such as many had never experienced before."[46]

Despite growing educational fervor, three long years passed before the dream became reality. In 1941, under the leadership of Executive Secretary L. R. Ennis, the Education Board purchased a beautiful home at 3609 Richland Avenue for $15,000. Free Will Baptist Bible School opened September 15, 1942, with nine students and Georgia pastor L. C. Johnson as the school's first president.

Welch, Johnson, and countless other Free Will Baptists passionate about Christian education laid the college foundation well. Nearly 75 years and two name changes later, the college continues to thrive. More than a century after John L. Welch became the sole student of the "failed" Free Will Baptist University, Welch College, the college that became his namesake, continues to produce pastors, missionaries, teachers, and professionals dedicated to the mission of *serving Christ, His Church, and His world through biblical thought and life.*[47]

GLOBAL IMPACT: FREE WILL BAPTIST MISSIONS

(CHRONOLOGICAL NARRATIVE)

From the beginning, the National Association of Free Will Baptists has been characterized by an emphasis on missions. In the denomination's first item of business, delegates voted to support the work of individual Free Will Baptist missionaries. The move came on the heels of a heartfelt lecture by Thomas (Pop) Willey on "Foreign Mission Work in South America."

In reality, the global work was already well under way. Laura Belle Barnard had already set sail for India with a promise of support from the Eastern General Conference. Thomas and Mabel (Mom and Pop) Willey reached the field within the year, working for a term in Panama before political unrest led them to Cuba in 1941. Bessie Yeley was already hard at work in Venezuela. Though she did not affiliate with the denomination until 1938, most of her financial support stemmed from Free Will Baptist churches in Ohio.

Although few written records exist from the early years, missions efforts grew steadily under the leadership of Winford Davis and Ken Turner of Missouri. The hard-working pair crisscrossed the denomination, raising awareness and funds.

In 1941, delegates to the National Association in Drumright, Oklahoma, approved a constitution and bylaws and formed the Foreign Missions Board. In the decades that followed, denominational efforts in world evangelism took flight. Paul and Nelle Woolsey joined Laura Belle Barnard in India. Dan and Trula Cronk and Carlilse and Marie Hanna soon followed. The work in Cuba continued to thrive, and in 1943, under the leadership of the Willeys, Cuban Christians formed the Free Will Baptist Association of Cuba.

By the time Raymond Riggs became secretary-treasurer in 1950, it was clear a full-time director was needed. Three years later, Riggs opened an office in the new headquarters building in Nashville, Tennessee. He began a campaign of awareness, publishing books and pamphlets including Miss Barnard's *His Name Among the Nations,* and *A Modern Jonah* by Paul Woolsey. Riggs also produced a 16mm film, *Letter to Melitino,* which told the powerful story of the Willey's work in Cuba and the birth of the Cedars of Lebanon Bible Institute.

As awareness blossomed, support expanded, and the scope of missions increased. Fields opened in Japan, West Africa, Brazil, Uruguay, France, and Spain. Stateside operations also expanded to support the growing needs of missionaries. During the early 1960s, Jerry Ballard began to produce literature and filmstrips to inform the denomination of each important milestone. He became the first editor of *HeartBeat* magazine, which captured the stories and images of the denomination's massive global undertaking.

By 1975, 93 missionaries were hard at work in nine countries, with the promise of new fields to come. Despite the early success, Laura Belle Barnard's words echo through the years:

> *The work of evangelism can never be finished as long as it is regarded as a secondary obligation. It is our primary duty in this Gospel age to do the work which Thou gavest us to do. Oh Lord, teach us to strive—by purposeful, intelligent prayer, by laying upon the altar our tithes and sacrificial offerings, by*

offering ourselves and our children to go as missionaries in the will of God, by keeping the work of missions prominent in our homes and church life. Amen![48]

Source Notes

INTRODUCTION: LEARNING FROM LUKE

1. As noted above, this book draws upon the collective wisdom of twelve individuals, experts with experience in history, documentation and preservation, writing, printing, marketing, and design. Their input, gathered through a series of interviews is quoted heavily throughout the book without separate notation. Transcripts of all interviews are available upon request. Learn more about these contributors in *Appendix A.*

CHAPTER ONE

2. Keith Burden. "The Importance of Keeping Records." *Contact:* October 2003, 8.

3. Donald L. Hughes. *Capturing Faith: How to Research and Write a Local Church History.* San Diego: Theatron Books, 2011, 14–24.

4. Jack Williams. "The Midnight Writer." *Contact:* Briefcase, March 1981, 5.

5. Jack Williams. "The Day We Lost 600 Churches." Presented at the request of the Commission for Theological Integrity at the 1994 Welch College Bible Conference: March 9, 1994. Quote taken from the handwritten manuscript.

CHAPTER TWO

6. Hughes. *Capturing Faith,* 28.

7. Ibid. 28.

CHAPTER THREE

8. Keith Burden. "Developing a Handbook for Church Clerks Among Oklahoma Free Will Baptist Churches." Research Project: Moody Bible Institute, 2001, 6–10.

9. Keith Burden. "The Importance of Keeping Records."

10. Keith Burden. "Brother Waldo." *ONE Magazine:* December–January 2018, 54.

11. Ibid.

CHAPTER FOUR

12. Hughes. *Capturing Faith,* 41.

13. Jack Williams. "Research Makes a Difference." Excerpts from a speech prepared for the 1981 Free Will Baptist Writer's Conference.

14. Hughes. *Capturing Faith,* 43–50.

15. Williams. "Research Makes a Difference."

16. Ibid.

17. Ibid.

18. Ibid.

19. Arthur L. Walker, Jr. "Interpreting Church Minutes." *The Alabama Historian.* Special Issue on Preserving and Writing Church History, April 1987.

20. Ibid.

21. Ibid.

22. Irma R. Cruse. "Using Oral Interviews." *The Alabama Historian.* Special Issue on Preserving and Writing Church History, April 1987.

23. Quentin Porch. "The Use of Secular Newspapers in Writing Church History." *The Alabama Historian.* Special Issue on Preserving and Writing Church History, April 1987.

24. Ibid.

CHAPTER FIVE

25. Jack Williams. "Research Makes a Difference."

26. Hughes. *Capturing Faith,* 73. Hughes acknowledges that restricting writing to a set outline flies in the face of the recent trend of "free writing" but insists the benefits of an outline when writing history are too significant to discard the method.

27. Ibid. 72–76.

28. Jack Williams. "Research Makes a Difference."

29. Hughes. *Capturing Faith*, 87.

30. Jack Williams. "Research Makes a Difference."

31. Hugh C. Bailey. "Baptist History Statistical Tables." *The Alabama Historian.* Special Issue on Preserving and Writing Church History, April 1987.

APPENDIX C: INTELLECTUAL PROPERTY

32. Glossary. United States Trademark Office. Accessed 18 February 2018: https://www.uspto.gov/learning-and-resources/glossary#sec-i.

33. Information adapted from the United States Patent and Trademark Office and Copyright websites: https://www.uspto.gov, https://copyright.gov/what-is-copyright/.

APPENDIX D: HISTORICAL VIGNETTES

34. Robert E. Picirilli. "What's in a Name?" FWBHistory.com: May 2016. Accessed 3 March 2018: https://fwbhistory.com/?p=516.

35. Norman Allen Baxter. *History of the Freewill Baptists; a Study in New England Separatism.* Rochester, NY: American Baptist Historical Society, 1957.

36. Ibid. 39.

37. David Marks. *The Life of David Marks.* Limerick: Printed at the Office of the Morning Star, 1831, 104-105.

38. Steve Hasty. "The Whirlwind Evangelist." FWBHistory.com. Accessed 6 March 2018: http://fwbhistory.com/?p=307.

39. Damon C. Dodd. *The Free Will Baptist Story.* Nashville: Executive Department of the National Association of Free Will Baptists, 1956, 124.

40. Clara A. Ricker. "The Thank-Offering Service." *The Free Baptist Woman's Missionary Society, 1873-1921.* Providence: Free Baptist Woman's Missionary Society, 80. Quoting Dean Fenn of the Harvard Divinity School.

41. Danny Baer. "Do Free Will Baptists Still Wash Feet?" *ONE Magazine:* February-March 2016, 46. Baer explores in some detail the current statistics regarding feetwashing among denominational churches.

42. Mary R. Wisehart. *Sparks Into Flame: A History of the Woman's National Auxiliary Convention of the National Association of Free Will Baptists, 1935-1985.* Nashville: Woman's National Auxiliary Convention, 1985, 32.

43. *The Free Baptist Woman's Missionary Society, 1873-1921.* Providence: Free Baptist Woman's Missionary Society. General historical information about the early efforts of Free Will Baptist women comes from this volume.

44. Wisehart. *Sparks Into Flame*, 58.

45. Ibid. 58.

46. Minutes of the Third Session of the National Association of Original Free Will Baptists. Clinchco, Virginia: *The Morning Herald Press*, 1939, 3. Accessed 12 February 2018: http://fwbhistory.com/wp-content/uploads/2013/03/1939.pdf.

47. Eric K. Thomsen. "John Welch and the Free Will Baptist University." *ONE Magazine:* December-January 2016. Learn more about the early developments of Free Will Baptist education in this expanded text.

48. Laura Belle Barnard. *His Name Among All Nations.* Nashville: Board of Foreign Missions, 1946, 197.

ALSO AVAILABLE FROM RANDALL HOUSE

MORE ON THE FASCINATING HISTORY OF FREE WILL BAPTISTS

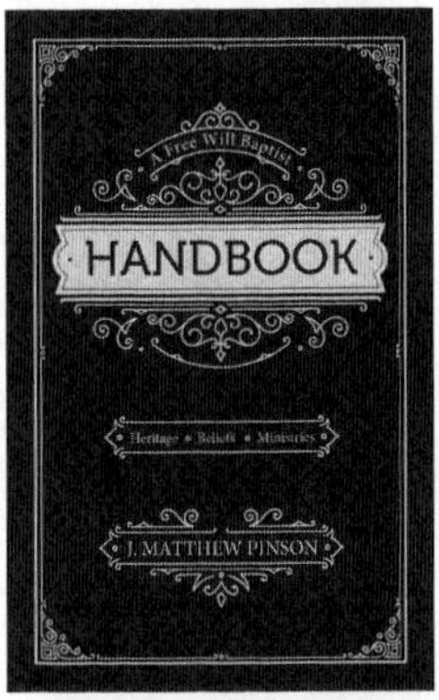

A Free Will Baptist Handbook (2nd Ed.)
J. Matthew Pinson

Learn who Free Will Baptists are, where they originated, what they believe, and what God is doing through them.

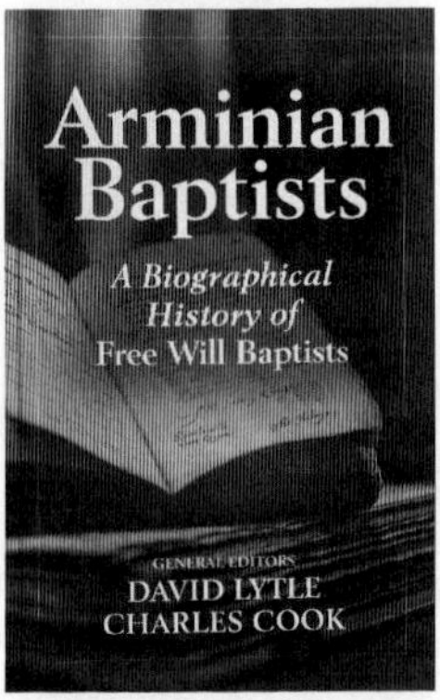

Arminian Baptists: A Biographical History of Free Will Baptists
Charles Cook and David Lytle, Editors

Read short biographies of key historical figures, starting with 17th century English General Baptists and continuing to the present day.

Free Will Baptist History: Exploring Our Origins and Identity
Robert E. Picirilli

Explore fascinating moments and milestones from Free Will Baptist history. Also from Picirilli: *Little Known Chapters in Free Will Baptist History.*

Meet the Author

Eric K. Thomsen has been the managing editor of *ONE Magazine* since 2005. He spent the ten previous years at Randall House Publications, serving at various times as event planner, editor, copy editor, and manager of marketing and design. A member of the Free Will Baptist Historical Commission, he is the creator and curator of FWBHistory.com, an online repository of historical books, records, and documents. Eric served as the general editor of *Free Will Baptist Convention Sermons* (2011) and authored *Honoring Our Heritage*, a 2011 documentary exploring the 400-year history of Free Will Baptists. He has served as a board member for the Evangelical Press Association (2012–2018), also serving as vice-president and president of the organization. A 1995 graduate of Welch College, Eric completed the M.A. in Theology and Ministry at Welch in 2018. He and his wife Jennifer are members of Bethel Church near Ashland City, Tennessee. They have one daughter, Victoria (Cody) Matlock.

ERIC@NAFWB.ORG
@ERICKTHOMSEN
FWBHISTORY.COM
ONEMAG.ORG